These stories have been collected and edited

by

Ruth Trueblood Eckes

© Copyright 1995

Cover: Jack Christensen

First Edition

ISBN 0-945433-37-9

Printed by
Heritage Quest Press
220 Bridge St. S.W. (P.O. Box 24)
Orting, Washington, 98360-0024

DEDICATION

This book is dedicated to railroaders everywhere and to my three grandchildren: Kyle Eckes, Danny Seidman and Alexandra Seidman.

Additional copies of Rail Tales may be purchased by sending $15.00 plus $2.00 shipping and handling to:

RAIL TALES
35603 Military Rd. S.
Auburn, WA 98001

Washington State residents please enclose 8.2% state sales tax.

ACKNOWLEDGEMENTS

The idea for RAIL TALES was born in 1991, at a meeting of the MORSE TELEGRAPH CLUB (MTC) — EVERGREEN CHAPTER in Fife, Washington.

In answer to my suggestion that day that someone should collect railroad stories before it was too late, they said, "Great idea Ruth. You do it!"

I immediately started contacting retirees for their stories and some of the first contributions I received were generously submitted from this group and I thank them for getting me started. Also the national MTC paper DOTS AND DASHES sent out word across the country and my telephone began to ring and the mailman brought me bulging envelopes filled with stories of the past.

As this collection of stories grew larger than could be printed in one book, I reflected on the great number of persons who submitted their stories for publication; well known railroad photographers who let me use their pictures; and all the people who had given me aid in one form or another.

The phone calls from across the nation brought me instant friends who had worked on other railroads and although I have never met them, their additional phone calls and letters provided many a laugh or groan as we discussed our experiences with one another.

The end results were stories of different aspects of railroading submitted by retirees who worked the great railroads of the past. Their stories were of first jobs, hard working conditions, unusual experiences and danger. Some of the stories are short — moments in a lifetime, but strong enough to be remembered.

I must especially cite Jack Christensen, Burlington Northern engineer who let us use one of his beautiful railroad paintings for our cover; James M. Fredrickson, retired Burlington Northern Railroad dispatcher, for wonderful pictures and cheerfully trying to keep rail history straight in my mind; Albert Farrow, retired Burlington Northern engineer and photographer for the many pictures I used; Warren Wing, author of railroad books, for pictures and encouragement along the way; Bud Emmons, (President of the Tacoma MTC), for pictures and materials I would never otherwise have had the use of; Jean Crittenden, dear friend, who learned more about railroading than she wanted to know while conducting a patient search for typos and correct punctuation; and of course all those authors who shared their experiences for our enjoyment and history of railroading between 1910 and 1980.

I must also mention my husband, Ed, who doled out patience by the carload and continuous help as I struggled to find stories. My son-in-law, Marc Seidman, designed the RAIL TALES logo and steered me through the computer jungle. My sister, Linda McPhaden, came up with the name, RAIL TALES for the book. Each deserves credit in this project. If I have left anyone out, please forgive me as it was not intentional. I am truly grateful to all those who helped.

❧ ERRATA ❧

- Page VII should read Fred T. Moser
- Page VIII, Photo 24 should read James M. Fredrickson, as well as Page 93, Photo 38 and Page 94, Photo 37, both of which should be credited to Jim
- Page 154 should read Don Roadifer

Please accept my apology for the printing errors-

- Ruth Trueblood Eckes

TABLE OF CONTENTS

23. Blackie Moser, Engineer.

INTRODUCTION

Railroads in the United States got their start in the year 1831. With them was born a new species, the "Railroad Man." They were a breed apart. They moved at speeds unheard of, and until fairly recently unrivaled. For years nothing equaled the trains in size and every boy's dream was connected to the steam locomotive.

Their life style was unique. The danger of their profession in the early times was beyond present day imagination. In 1890, the first year anyone bothered to count, 2690 were known killed. Still, they came to fill the jobs and move the trains. Because of the hours they worked, the constant travel, no home life, and the danger, they became unbelievably clannish. Sufficient unto themselves, if you will. They even developed virtually their own language. They were a cross section of the land and included every sort of hero and villain known.

Today, those people are gone; their stories either lost or recorded in the pages of time; but "Rail Tales" are still being written by the men of today.

These are the stories of a way of life written by the men and women who lived them. No apology is offered for the language used or for some of the colloquial expressions. We often started very young with limited education and devoted our whole working life of forty or fifty years to just one job and location.

These stories are a sampling of our lives taken from all parts of the land, and we hope you enjoy the sharing.

Fred F. (Blackie) Moser
January 29, 1993

24. James R. Fredrickson at Model Railroad Show, Pacific Science Center in Seattle, Washington. *Photo, Ed Eckes.*

FORWARD

Change. Never ending change. That is the story of the railroad over the past fifty years. Gone are steam locomotives and the water tank and coaling towers needed to support them. Gone is the click of the telegraph and abandoned wires dangle from the telephone poles. Cabooses are following the small-town station into oblivion. Railroad employment has dwindled dramatically and customers now use "800" numbers or FAX machines to distant centers instead of dropping in on the office by the tracks down town.

Railroading has always been a glamorous profession on the surface, much hard work and even danger behind the scenes. "The way it was" before technology took over is a story that must be told while those who were there are still around to tell it.

Ruth Trueblood Eckes grew up in a railroad family and became a "rail" herself. Her father was a conductor and she went from high school to telegraph school to prepare for a career as telegrapher for the Northern Pacific. Ruth had a trackside seat at the peak of the railroad transformation from people oriented to computer oriented. Most importantly, Ruth has a deep sense of the value of history and she become dedicated to recording first hand the stories of those who made railroading their life. This book is the remarkable result of her efforts.

J. M. Fredrickson, retired telegrapher and
dispatcher for the Northern Pacific and
Burlington Northern Railroad.

#39. Bud Emmons, telegraph demonstration at Pacific Science Center Model Railroad Show, 1992 in Seattle, Washington. *Photo, Ed Eckes*

MY, OH MY, WHAT A LIFE!
By Bud Emmons - Tacoma, Washington

My poor ol' mom and dad surely got bounced around with dad's railroad career. They met at the Glencoe, Minnesota Milwaukee railroad station. She came to pick up a package; he was working afternoon shift as an extra telegrapher.

After but a few dates, dad was shipped off to Webster, South Dakota as extra train dispatcher. Their courtship consisted of a stack of letters and postcards.

My mother (Della Gould) came from well-to-do parents in the town of Glencoe on the Chicago Milwaukee main line, about one hour west of Minneapolis. She had a BA degree from the University of Minnesota; he had an eighth grade education from Lakeville, Minnesota. He learned telegraphy by hanging around the Milwaukee depot, sweeping out, filling oil lamps and doing other things that the depot agent should have been doing.

Dad's christened name was A. B., which is enough to give anyone an inferiority complex. His sister liked the name Allan so that sort of stuck. Around 1915 dad was working at a telegraph station in Montana and was filling out papers that called for a middle name. Looking up at the window and waiting for his orders was Conductor Burdett. Dad said, "Your name sounds good enough to me, so from now on my middle name is going to be Burdett."

Dad and mother were married in Glencoe. Dad's parents did not attend as they thought the affair was above their status. They were just farmers and mother's parents owned most of the town.

Later on, dad got a short leave of absence from his dispatcher's job at Webster on the Milwaukee Railroad. Mom and dad went on a honeymoon trip to Niagara Falls. This was September, 1913, and this was the proper place to go for a honeymoon.

On return to Webster with his bride, dad found his job occupied by a relative of the superintendent, so he had to take a cut in salary and an operator's job further west.

1

#51. Bud Emmons, Lester depot telegraph bay about 1978, after the telegraph instruments were removed. *Photo, Bud Emmons.*

RAIL TALES

My sister was born in Aberdeen, South Dakota the next year. The two now had a small baby and were shipped even further west to Montevideo, Bird Island, Harlowton, Roundup, Three Forks, Deer Lodge, Butte, Missoula · · · always moving further west where there was a job and work.

Dad worked twelvehour shifts seven days a week. Mother tried to get a few nice things, but mostly they lived out of apple boxes.

One day in 1917, on dad's shift as dispatcher at Missoula, there was a bad train wreck. Dad said the train crew overlooked an order. It didn't matter who was at fault, everyone on duty or who had a part in the accident was fired outright, without any hearing. The superintendent was foaming at the mouth and in those years his word was law.

The family loaded up their few belongings, and hearing Seattle might have job openings, headed further west again. Dad did get a job with the Transcontinental Freight Bureau. World War I was in progress but he was underweight and too short to be drafted. They lucked out on that one for a change, but that job lasted only a short time. Dad took out a loan and bought a car for a taxi and spent his time ferrying troops from Seattle to Fort Lewis.

Finally, there was a job opening as an extra dispatcher on the Northern Pacific Railway. That was the year 1920, and he got one or two days a month at first, with most of his time spent out on the line as extra operator on the mountain. Ravensdale, Kanaskat, Eagle Gorge, Lester, Stampede — he worked them all.

In 1922, he bid in third trick at Eagle Gorge, one of the most beautiful places in the state of Washington. There were living quarters furnished by the company and the Green River which ran right beside the station was full of mountain trout. This wasn't work, dad had finally found paradise.

Mother wasn't much of a sport, and stayed in Seattle in a rented apartment. On weekends she took my sister and me on the train to Eagle Gorge. I was only three, but still remember the great time I had throwing rocks in the river, playing with the dog, Tricksy, and watching the mammoth trains just outside the

3

#27. Allan B. Emmons, dispatcher on Milwaukee Railroad in Webster, South Dakota, 1913. *Bud Emmons collection*

station door. The smell of the oil lamps, cigar smoke and the sound of the telegraph instruments were firmly imbedded in my mind.

By 1924, dad finally got on steady as third trick dispatcher working "the mountain" territory. He was unable to hold a day job, and then came the Depression. Seattle and Tacoma dispatcher offices were consolidated and dad was out of a job again.

The Tacoma dispatchers were a bunch of 'old heads' (they had lots of seniority) so dad had to pick up a day here and there at telegraph stations, just as he did when he first went to work on the Northern Pacific.

In 1932, he had enough seniority to hold third trick Yakima Yard telegraph and I kept him company on weekends and all summer. Hunting and fishing were good there. Mom didn't care for the tiny house dad and another operator, Cal Zimmerman, were renting for $12 a month, but I thought it was great. I did a lot of swimming in the Yakima River and rode the trains whenever possible.

In 1933, dad bid in third trick Stampede, which was closer to home and was considered a good job on which to save money. Stampede was located just on the west side of the Cascade summit, where during the winter snow was from eight to ten feet deep and rotary snow plows were used to keep the pass open.

Skiing, hunting and fishing were wonderful. I spent every minute I could there, taking the train from Seattle on Friday night and returning on No. 5 Sunday evening. Mr. Black was the gruff, old conductor on trains 4 and 5. He knew my pass number and never asked me to present it. I was on the train so much of the time that I can still remember the number on that pass — 55505.

Everyone riding trains 3, 4, 5, and 6 were "deadheads"— that was what pass riders were called. Right on the pass was printed, NOT GOOD ON TRAINS NOS. 1 AND 2, which was the NORTH COAST LIMITED and it had to be a real emergency to ride free.

I was able to spend three summers there on the hill, learning enough telegraphy to operate the station with no problem.

5

#26. A.B. Emmons, Milwaukee telegrapher in 1909 and later chief dispatcher on Northern Pacific Railway in Tacoma, Washington. *Bud Emmons collection.*

Judge Realyea was the second trick operator and Lloyd Kalander was first trick. They didn't care if I bugged them all day. I helped wash respirators, throw the double track switch, take the staff out of the machine, and fill oil lamps, so I guess I was some help around there.

Dad finally was able to get some work in the Tacoma dispatcher's office and sometime during 1935, bid in the third trick mountain job. He lived in a hotel room in Tacoma for about a year and in 1936, we sold the house near Green Lake in Seattle and moved to Tacoma.

Poor ol' pop never did get a day job, he went from trick dispatcher to night chief dispatcher, and worked that frantic job with all the troop trains and high priority trains during World War II.

He had a very severe heart attack on the job in 1945, and was off work about six months. He came out of it pretty well, but never again had the energy or drive he once had. He was one darn good train dispatcher and also a good Morse telegrapher. He never used a bug, never owned one. He had a "fist" anyone could read.

And what was mom doing all these years? Having lived along the Lewis and Clark trail on their way west from station to station, she became interested in the expedition. She gathered material, studied journals, and wrote a book in story form as seen by Sacajawea, the Shoshone Indian girl captured by the Mandan tribe. Paramount made a movie, "The Far Horizons," from mom's novel.

She became very interested in the Pacific Northwest Indians and wrote the story, "Leshi, Chief of the Nisquallies." One of her other novels was about the first wagon train over the Cascades into the Nisqually Delta area.

For many years mom was on the board of directors of the Washington State Historical Society. Her friends included governors, senators, bank presidents, and she even had correspondence with presidents of the United States.

For all of that, she only made a couple thousand dollars in those years of work. Dad said she spent more money on typewriter paper and ribbons then she made!

#25. Della (Gould) Emmons and children, Kathryn and Bud. Picture taken at NP depot, Stampede in 1933. *Bud Emmons collection.*

My father retired in 1955, holding the position of Chief Dispatcher. Here again, he was CDT, but then again he wasn't. Austin W. Ackley, the officially assigned Chief, was on sick leave for about two years. Dad was officially appointed Chief, then Ackley said he wanted to go back to work, but never did. Ackley had a seniority date two weeks ahead of dad's and this cost dad his company pension check. He probably could have put in a claim against the company and won his earned pension, but he wasn't that type of person.

My father died in 1958 at age seventy-one. He did get one airplane ride to California. He always wanted to fly. Mother lived a very active life alone until she was eighty-seven, keeping up her writing in historical journals and working with State and Indian rights. My, oh my, what a life!

THE BOOMERS

By Jerry Pratt - Milton, Washington

Back in the early days of World War II, new faces began to appear in the Northern Pacific Railroad yard office in Tacoma, Washington. Among them was a "boomer" switchman and his daughter. Their names are unknown.

At that time George Cobb, second trick Chief Clerk, was in charge at the Bay Yard in Tacoma.

In those days, yard clerks were given cards designating where the cars were to be switched and it was the yard clerks' job to go out and attach them to the cars

Old George, gave this "boomer daughter" a handful of cards and instructed her to go over to the "Old Side" where the Amtrak Depot is now located and card the cars.

Quite some time later she returned to the yard office, handed the cards to George and said, "You know what you can do with these, don't you?"

If the boomers didn't like the job they were assigned to do, they were quick to tell you about it and move on!

28. Peter Martin Johnson about 1900. *Eldon E. Johnson collection.*

RAIL TALES

PETER MARTIN JOHNSON
By Eldon Johnson - Fallbrook, California

A wiry, erect man with prominent ears, piercing hazel eyes and an angular nose, Peter sat at the telegraph desk in the bay window, copying a train order. He wrote with an indelible pencil on a pad of green tissue. A cloth cap sat squarely on his head, the visor casting a shadow over the upper half of his face. He held a pipe with a curved stem in one corner of his mouth. As the bar of the telegraph sounder danced to the hand of the train dispatcher, the clatter of the instrument resounded from the walls of the railroad office. The telegraph desk was a counter about two and one half feet deep and eight feet long, built into the bay window. Most railroad stations of the time had bay windows, so the operator had only to lean forward in the chair and look in either direction to see if a train was approaching.

Absorbed in copying the order word for word, letter by letter, Peter forgot to puff on his pipe. So far, he had written: No. 54 take siding . . . . There was little movement in the high-ceilinged green painted room except for the pendulum of the Seth Thomas clock, the bar of the clacking sounder and an iron handle that swung at the end of a chain descending from a pulley mounted at the top of the bay window. The chain continued outside through a hole in the woodwork, and was fastened at its far end to a lever on the train order signal. The signal was a red oval of sheet steel with two white-ringed holes in it, suspended from a wooden bracket over the platform.

When the dispatcher called, "BR" (Brooks) on the telegraph, Peter opened the key and responded, "BR." Then the dispatcher said, "19" and Peter slipped the iron handle from its catch. This let the train order signal swing of its own weight to the stop position. A train could not legally proceed beyond such a signal without the dispatcher's written authority. The written authority came by telegraph, not by mail.

If Peter had been following the rules to the letter he would have taken a yellow flag outside and hung it beneath the signal before he copied the order, for the order was of a type meant to be delivered to a moving train. But Peter long ago developed the habit of displaying the yellow flag — or at night a yellow lantern — last, after the order was complete and the dispatcher issued a clearance. That way, if the situation got to "nip and tuck," the engineer of the approaching train would see the stop signal and prepare to stop, giving Peter more time to get ready to make the delivery.

He knew that should the train arrive before the order and clearance were completed it would have to stop and wait. He also knew the engineer might complain and perhaps profanely remind Peter that without the yellow flag or lantern the signal called for a "31" order, which needed the signature of the engineer before the dispatcher would declare it complete. But stopping a train at the signal was preferable to missing the delivery and having the train back up to get the order.

The telegraph sounder was mounted in a wooden resonator on top an iron pedestal. Besides the sounder, the telegraph desk held two telegraph keys with corresponding relays; a number of pads of train order tissue set up in manifold with carbon paper; a disused stylus — he preferred the indelible pencil; a pad or two of clearance forms; a stack of Postal Telegraph message blanks; a tray of straight pins with which to fasten orders and clearances together; an assortment of pencils; a brass ashtray with a knocker-knob in the center; a glass paper weight; a spindle on which to file copies of the orders; a kerosene lamp with a clean chimney; a fly swatter; a copy of Collier's magazine; a pile of freight tariffs waiting to be filed; a pair of soiled and worn gloves; a green celluloid eye shade and a can of Prince Albert tobacco. He carried matches, large wooden ones, in the lower right hand pocket of his vest. In the lower left hand pocket he carried a 21-jewel Illinois watch attached to a thin gold chain secured in a buttonhole.

After the dispatcher had signed the order with the chief dispatcher's initials ("W.W.W."), Peter repeated the text exactly as written.

The dispatcher then responded with "Com" (complete) and the time of day, which Peter wrote in the proper blank at the bottom. Opening the telegraph key he sent: "Clear No. 54 with 19 No. 34." There were no other applicable orders.

The dispatcher said: "OK clear No. 54 with 19 order No. 34" and gave the time and the chief dispatcher's initials.

Peter recorded this on the clearance form and then pinned a clearance to each of two copies of the train order.

Taking the delivery hoops down from their place on the wall, he slipped the folded orders into the clips provided, took the yellow flag from its rack under the ticket window ledge and went outside. No. 54 was whistling for a crossing a half mile away.

Well, before the engine reached the depot, the yellow flag was in position and Peter stood holding one of the hoops at arm's length, within reach of the engineer's arm. He had learned long ago that it was wise to grip the shaft of the hoop with both hands firmly, so that the rush of air set up by the locomotive could not twist the hoop in his grasp or otherwise move it out of the engineer's reach. Just as the engineer's arm entered the hoop, Peter let go. The engineer slipped the orders from the clip and tossed the hoop back to the platform. As the end of the train approached Peter held up the second hoop, lower now, to catch the arm of the brakeman standing on the rear step of the caboose. The brakeman removed the orders, dropped the hoop at the end of the platform and waved at Peter, who waved back.

In the office Peter hung up the hoops, restored the flag to its rack, sat down at the telegraph desk and opened the key. "OS, BR" he sent. (OS stands for order sheet, on which the dispatcher records the movement of trains.)

After the dispatcher responded with "DI," Peter telegraphed: "No. 53 by 3:32."

The dispatcher acknowledged receipt. It was 3:36 on a warm summer afternoon. He left the signal in stop position to serve as a block signal. Although there were no trains scheduled to arrive even within an hour, it was wise to follow the rules. Extra trains sometimes ran unexpectedly. The signal could be cleared at 3:47, or fifteen minutes after departure of a train. If a following train should be stopped by the signal, Peter

29. Northern Pacific station at Vining, Minnesota, circa 1900. It was here that my father, Peter Martin Johnson, learned the railroad business beginning about 1898. Identities of agent or onlookers are unknown. The newspaper displayed by the paper boy is the Fergus Falls Journal. *Artist: Eldon Johnson*.

would have to ask the dispatcher for authority to issue a clearance before it could proceed.

Turning to his typewriter, a battered L. C. Smith, Peter began to type freight bills, one for each of a sheaf of waybills. For the few waybills that did not carry freight charges, he consulted his tariff file before typing in the amount. A railroad agent had to be many things. It was necessary, someone once said, to have the mind of a Philadelphia lawyer in order to make sense of the tariffs. The freight had been delivered to the stores by the drayman some hours earlier. Tomorrow, Peter would carry the bills downtown and collect from each of the storekeepers in turn. Or he might send his son, Eldon, whom was now twelve and quite old enough to help out with such things.

In 1895, Peter hung around the depot at Vining, Minnesota, excited with the prospect of working in such an interesting and mobile industry as the railroad. Later, he went to business school in the Twin Cities, thinking of someday becoming a railroad official. Upon graduation, he went to work for the Minnesota Transfer Railway at New Brighton, hoping to stay with a promising company. But the rheumatism in his hips worsened, and the doctors advised more exercise and a change of climate. His left leg had been shorter at birth and had never caught up with his right one.

He went to Montana in 1908 to herd sheep for a season in the Gallatin Valley. In 1909, he settled in Roundup, north of Billings, and with a partner opened a house painting business. They called it Buckley Paint Company for a reason having nothing to do with names, but with a ribald phrase his partner was in the habit of shouting after he had drunk too many bottles of beer.

Peter wrote to the division superintendent of the Northern Pacific at Livingston, Montana sometime in 1909: "I am looking for a job as agent. Am a good station man of varied experience. Started out on the Northern Pacific in 1898, working on the second district, Minnesota Division about three years as helper, agent and operator. Have been away from railroad work entirely since December 1907, when I resigned from night operator job at Twin City Stockyards, Minnesota Transfer Railway, C. S. Espennet, agent." The reply to his letter was unfavorable. Later he wrote again, with the same results.

In the fall of 1911 he went home to the farm near Henning, Minnesota and subsequently hired out to the Soo Line Railway. Six months later, when he was working as night operator at Alexandria, Minnesota he married Ellen Emelia Emberetson, whom his sisters had known since her family moved to Henning in 1906. She was twenty-seven, having been born in 1884, and had been teaching school in various places. Peter taught a term of school himself, at sixteen, with only a grammar school education. Ellen had gone to normal school. They were married in Henning on May 15, 1912. Soon afterwards they moved to Ardoch, North Dakota, where he worked as agent for the Soo Line, and his first child, Elia Meredith was born, on May 5, 1913. The following October they moved to Orleans, Minnesota. His second child, Eldon Elliot was born there November 16, 1916.

He preferred to be farther south where the winters were less severe. Orleans was in northwestern Minnesota, situated where you could see forever on a clear day, and the snow buried the town at least once each winter.

In 1920, he put in his bid for and was awarded the agency at Almora, just south of Henning. They moved there, glad to be back in their old 'stamping grounds.' In 1923, the railroad decided to close the Almora agency. It was the beginning of a retrenchment that thereafter never ceased. They moved to Alexandria in June of 1923, back to the night trick again.

In September he bid in Newfolden, north of Thief River Falls, and moved back into severe winters. It was by no means as far south as he wanted to be, but it was the best he could do for the present.

His rheumatism was as troubling as ever. He was at ease only in the full heat of summer. He had long since given up any thought of becoming a railroad official. He couldn't stomach the politics involved. He was a forthright man, and was restricted enough in that regard as an ordinary agent. He had discovered that there was deceit involved in mere survival.

Nobody wanted to deal with the truth. People expected comfort, no honesty.

He could hear Ellen getting something ready for supper upstairs in the kitchen. The living rooms overhead were the same as those in every other small-town depot. There was a medium-sized kitchen with a pantry, a living room, two bedrooms, one of them barely large enough for a single bed, and a chimney closet in which he had installed a sanitary toilet for use in winter. The rooms were cold in winter and hot in summer. But both he and Ellen had been brought up in drafty farm houses. He planned to have a comfortable home someday, with central heating and running water. His expectations had dwindled until a decent place in which to spend his last years was all he hoped for. Before too long, the agent at Miltona, a small town north of Alexandria, was due to retire. By that time Peter should have enough seniority to bid it in. There were no living rooms there. Miltonia would be a good place to build a new house, a good place to settle down and enjoy themselves.

Opening the cash drawer beneath the ledge of the ticket window, he counted the money. He always spoke of the drawer as "till." He made up a remittance, slipping it, together with a remittance slip, into a manila envelope pre-addressed to a Minneapolis bank. Part of the currency was small, new and crisp, measuring about 2 1/2 x 6 inches. The banks had begun to issue the smaller sized notes on July 10, 1929. Before long, none of the old fashioned shin-plasters would be in circulation. In the meantime it was a nuisance to handle two sizes of paper money. After sewing a stitch with a stiff needle and cord through the envelope and contents, he lit a match and dropped a gob of molten wax on the knotted cord. He quickly stamped the wax with the official seal, wrote up the remittance in a register and left the register on the table, with the envelope inserted as a mark.

The remittance would be put on the eastbound night train, No. 110, and go to the Twin Cities as railroad mail. The express messenger would sign the register and hand it back to whoever met the train. Ellen was the caretaker but Peter usually did the work. The job was in his wife's name because

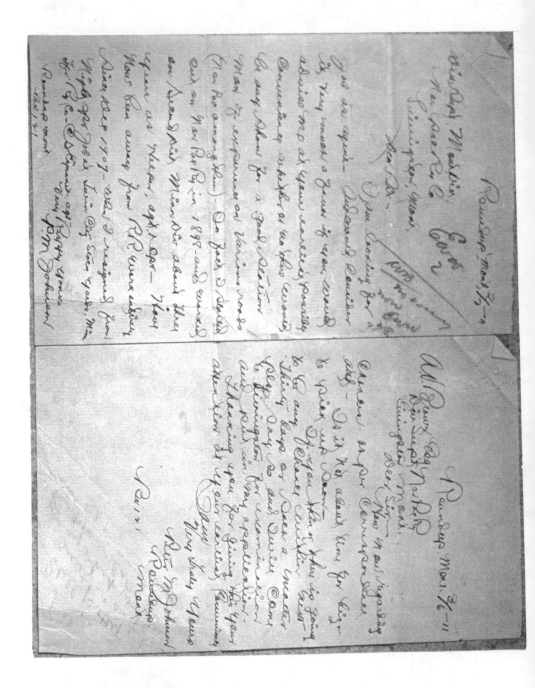

30. Two letters written by P.M. Johnson, in 1911, while looking for work on the Northern Pacific, after he had been in Montana for about three years herding sheep and painting houses. *Eldon Johnson Collection*

the agent couldn't legally hold it. No. 110, the Winnipeger, ran from Winnepeg, Manitoba, to Minneapolis and St. Paul, and was due about half an hour after midnight. Peter had grown accustomed to staying up late. He often spent the evening hours between seven and eleven playing rummy with the men at the pool hall, Sometimes, during vacations, Eldon met No. 110.

Brooks was a community of Frenchmen. Peter was Scandinavian and had been brought up a Lutheran but his outlook had been increasingly cosmopolitan. He was fluent in Norwegian; still he spoke English with only a trace of accent. His father had learned English in Norway, and his mother had come to America as a child. Ellen had no Norwegian accent to speak of, either. They made a point of speaking English around the children. It was an asset in this democratic land of opportunity. Ellen's sister, Emma, was a high school mathematics teacher in Duluth. Her sister, Julia, was a nurse at Nopeming sanitarium. Matilda was a chiropractor. Brother John was a lawyer.

Peter had no notable relatives on his side of the family, only his father, a Civil War veteran. His sisters had all married and became housewives. His brother, Otto, had worked as a railroad agent for a while before settling in Minneapolis and working for the Ford Motor Company. His elder brother, Henry, ran the home farm near Henning. Henry's first love was horses. His second was charming the women. Henry once had been a village marshal in Poplar, Montana. Just as Henry had been christened Charles Henry and later taken the middle name for a first, Peter had been christened Martin Peter. Now, everyone called him Pete or P.M. Some of the railroad men called him Afternoon.

Closing the ticket window, he shut and locked the door between the office and waiting room. It was five o'clock. He went into the freight house, walked around the platform truck and pulled the big door shut and hooked it. Now the only light came from a row of small panes above the closed door and through a like row over the south door. He seldom opened the south door, except when there was heavy freight to deliver to a waiting vehicle. The decor of the interior of the freight house was age-darkened wood. It was gloomy enough now to give a stranger difficulty in finding the way back to the office, but Peter was used to the dim reaches. He returned to the office.

Before going upstairs, he stood for a minute at the foot of the stairway looking out through the screen of the back door. He could see the lumber yard, Bruneau's Livery, the south side of the bank, Bruggeman's Cafe (which looked more like a house), a few homes, and the Catholic church towering over all. The street was dirt. It was not much of a town, but it was where he made a living.

He saw Eldon standing, holding his bicycle on the sidewalk at the bank corner, talking with a slight, young girl who Peter knew was Mildred Jackowski. When he watched Eldon, he often saw himself as he was at that age. Peter had had an eye for the girls too, for as long as he could remember.

Turning to go upstairs, he changed his mind and went back into the office. He picked up the Collier's magazine from the telegraph desk and went back to the stairway. Three steps and a landing, turn right; twelve steps and another landing, turn left. The steps were worn, and creaked in a number of tones. Halfway up he could hear the sounds of meat frying. At the top, his nose told him there would be pork chops for supper. He loved pork chops, especially the crisp-fried fat. At home on the farm there always had been plenty of fat meat, butter and cream. He loved rich, greasy food.

Ellen was sitting at the kitchen table with a copy of Woman's Home Companion spread out before her. She was no beauty but she had a certain defenseless, innocent look that had always attracted him. Her brown hair was done up in a knot at the back of her head. She had a small, pouting child's mouth. On their wedding night he had discovered that she was as innocent as she looked but by no means defenseless. She was never aggressive but neither was she long suffering. She looked up from her magazine and smiled.

"The chops smell good," he said, returning her smile.

He limped into the living room and turned on the radio. The depot had not been wired for electricity when they moved to

Brooks. He had wired it, at his own expense. The radio was new only a few months ago, a table model Philco with a cathedral top and a small metal-framed window above the tuning knob, through which could be seen the yellow, transparent dial. It was one of the earliest self-contained electric radios. Although battery radios had been available for some time, he had never bought one. He got all the news he wanted from newspapers and the telegraph. He felt that even an electric radio was extravagant. But after sundown many distant stations came in and there were programs to choose from. Ellen liked Ma Perkins.

Peter sat on the davenport. Filling and lighting his pipe, he opened the Collier's to a Damon Runyon story. After a while he heard Eldon downstairs, bringing his bicycle in through the back door, letting the screen door go shut with a bang. Then Eldon came noisily up the stairway, two steps at a time.

"What's for supper?" Eldon asked on his way through the kitchen.

"Pork chops. Can't you tell by the smell?" Ellen asked, not unkindly.

"Oh, yeah," Eldon replied, pulling a Wild West weekly out of the magazine rack.

Finishing the Damon Runyon story, Peter laid the magazine down and picked up the Minneapolis Star, a daily paper he had been taking for years. It was full of the Teapot Dome affair and still rehashed the Valentine's Day Massacre, in which seven gangsters were mowed down in Chicago. President Hoover said the economy was strong, and there was a story on the flight of the Graf Zeppelin.

Peter was a member of a labor union, the Order of Railroad Telegraphers, and a political liberal. He favored the Progressive Party and put little faith in the Republicans, such as Hoover. In 1928, he had voted for Alfred E. Smith, in 1924 for Robert M. LaFollette, and in 1920 for Cox and Roosevelt.

When the United States conscripted men aged twenty-one to thirty in 1917, Peter had been thirty-seven. He had been glad to be too old, but felt a little guilty about it. His younger brother, Otto, had been thirty-two. Otto had escaped the draft too.

Ellen's sister, Emma, said that Eldon resembled Charles Lindberg, -- Lindy, as everyone called the Minnesotan who had flown the Atlantic in 1927. There was some slight resemblance, but Peter doubted Eldon would ever do anything so demanding or hazardous. Eldon was more inclined toward the creative.

"Supper's ready," Ellen said from the kitchen doorway. "Eldon, wash your hands."

Peter Martin Johnson was the successful bidder for the Agency at Miltona, Minnesota in 1934. He built a modern home there in 1935. He died in 1946, at the age of sixty-eight.

CLOSE CALL

By Patrick Howe - Tacoma, Washington

As a retired engineer with the Burlington Northern Railroad and service seniority of forty-two years of railroading, I had many experiences of all kinds. I think the one that stands out in my mind was a trip in freight service one night on the waterfront in Seattle, Washington. The year was about 1979 or 1980.

I was traveling on the waterfront with my diesel power, moving at about ten miles per hour on the way to Stacy Street Yard to get our train. As I approached one of the crossings, a large gas truck coming from the opposite direction suddenly turned right in front of me. I put the brakes into emergency and jumped . . . running away from the impact.

The diesel power slid the gas truck sideways into a cement pillar of the Alaska Way Viaduct. My power cut a hole six feet in diameter in one of the truck trailers. The gas truck was carrying over 9000 gallons of gasoline and I had over 6000 gallons of diesel fuel. To the astonishment of the fire chief and me, there was no spark or explosion. The Chief said we would have lost about fifty feet of bridge and waterfront had it blown.

To this day I believe what my head brakeman said when he asked me if I went to church regularly.

I told him, "Yes."

He said, "You got your miracle all at once." AMEN.

RAIL TALES

A BRASS POUNDER'S INTRODUCTION TO
A LIFE LONG TRADE
By Herman A. Bergman - Canby, Oregon

My family: father, mother, brother Harold and I moved from Kulm, North Dakota after World War I to live the life of a "pioneer" family on the Standing Rock Indian Reservation, forty miles west of the Missouri River at a new little town, La Plant, South Dakota.

This town site was situated on treaty land set aside by the "Great White Father" in Washington, DC to be the home in perpetuity of the Cheyenne Sioux tribes. A few years before this, these were the tribes who so daringly had assisted in "Siouxing" General George Custer, whose command had invaded the Indian's land at Little Big Horn in Montana.

Our La Plant Indians were not too happily ensconced in this beautiful land that once was the home of seemingly unlimited herds of buffalo. The buffaloes at one time were their principal food source. Without equipment of any kind except a light farm wagon, these once proud warriors were told to be farmers. Some tried and marginally ranched but eventually had their hopes again dashed to the ground by an uncaring national congress who legislated the treaty rights of the Indians in favor of the Texas cattle barons. The Texans trailed immense herds of long-horned cattle that were soon displaced with short-horn breeds. The long-horns were also hunted into near extinction on the prairies.

Railroad builders had the backing of sympathetic congressmen to do their part in opening up the prairies and Indian land to settlement. The little cow-town of La Plant, South Dakota was the result of both factions; large ranches remained and branch lines of the Chicago, Milwaukee Railroad stabbed in all directions into virgin territory. They greedily gobbled all the Indian land. This opened it all to European settlers who cared not a whit for the rights and culture of the native population.

La Plant had a rather large depot with quarters upstairs for the agent and family. The agent, Mr. Booth, tried his best to

71. Southern Pacific station at Canby, Oregon.

24

teach his son Billy and me to telegraph. With such tutelage it wasn't long before we could pick up the gist of a message or train order. Maybe we made a nuisance of ourselves, but to a country bumpkin, the attention was great and we were welcomed. Mr. Booth probably realized the time to learn something is when your head isn't all clouded up with adult troubles.

Much railroad business originated and terminated at that depot. All the towns and vicinities received their supplies by rail. Whole train loads of steers and carloads of horses were loaded there, the result of the annual roundups of Diamond A cattle and DZ horse ranches output.

I don't know what caused the severe decline in business that in turn made the railroad shut down most of the stations on the branch line. The depression years put the finishing touches on our branch from Mobridge to Faith, South Dakota. It was a disaster causing most local businesses to close and families moved to greener pastures.

After we moved to Mobridge, South Dakota I found no opportunity to continue with telegraphy. The draft caught me in 1941 and I became a radio operator in a field artillery outfit at Fort Lewis, Washington. There I gained another love, the International Code.

After World War II, I applied to the Southern Pacific Railroad at Eugene, Oregon for a telegraph-operator job. I was hired and stayed with the Southern Pacific until retirement in 1976.

I barely used the telegraph except for messages and Western Union. I learned to type, which was most important in copying train orders and to operate the teletype. I finished my career as an agent. I figure I ran the full gamut of the rise and fall of a craft — the railroads, train orders and steam power.

C.T.C. (Centralized Traffic Control) was a wonderful advancement in technology, but just look at all the jobs eliminated and proud crafts so painstakingly learned — now useless knowledge.

After retiring from the Southern Pacific Railroad at Canby, Oregon, they closed the station and gave me the building. It was moved to another location and is now a museum with a few railroad artifacts. The old telegraphy and code are just as much artifacts as an inanimate railroad spike. In my case, it is only kept alive by a once a year visit with other members of the Morse Telegraph Club in Vancouver, Washington.

Jim Warren, telegrapher and Joe Rosati celebrating at Stampede, about 1917. *Jim Warren Collection*

RAIL TALES

I REMEMBER WHEN

By Jerry Johnson - Rockford, Illinois

I'm now ninety-three years old and I went to work on the Northern Pacific Railway on May 21, 1923 as a telegraph-operator and retired as Agent at Puyallup, Washington on September 7, 1965.

My first job was at Maywood, Washington in the Cascade foothills. It was a little "OS" job requiring hooping up orders to the trains. The railroad set out six cars of coal for use in the depot and the sleeping quarters where the operators stayed.

Later, I worked at Ravensdale, Kanaskat, Eagle Gorge, Auburn, Auburn Yard, Sumner and Kent. When I started, these stations were on the Seattle Division which ended at Ellensburg, Washington. They extended the division boundary to Yakima, Washington in 1932. After that, it was called the Tacoma Division East.

I remember Mrs. Fenner who worked third trick at Eagle Gorge. She would not let anyone climb the semaphore pole to take down the kerosene container to refill it. She insisted on doing the job herself. Those were the days of kerosene lamps in some of the depots.

I held third trick Stampede in 1928, and hooped up the staff and respirators to the engine crews on the trains and helper engines entering the long Stampede Tunnel. The staff gave authority to those going from double track to the single track through the tunnel and back to double track at Martin on the east side of the tunnel. The Rooks brothers had the job of blowing the smoke out of Stampede Tunnel with steam power and later electric motors were used. We lived in company quarters at Old Stampede.

When I worked third trick at Stampede, I hooped up the staff to an extra east on one particular night and there was an extra west coming up at Martin.

The fireman said, "Clear board."

But the head brakeman said, "YOU GOT A RED BOARD!"

The engineer said, "The fireman knows a clear board from a red board."

27

36. Northern Pacific Railway Hotel at Lester, Washington. Year unknown. *Courtesy of the Foothills Historical Society, Buckley, Washington.*

At that point the brakeman left the train. They hit the other train in the snowsheds at Martin and were locked together. The engines were two big Mallets.

While working third trick at Stampede, I had a little trouble. I had an order on the hook addressed to: All C&E Eastward trains (C&E means conductor and engineer). It concerned a flanger running against the current of traffic from Easton to Martin. There was an extra east out of Lester and I heard the operator "OS" (report) the train out of town and asked Dispatcher George Farrington to clear the extra east on this order.

He said, "I will tell you when to clear the extra east."

I forgot all about this order and rang the staff machine for a staff, leaving the order hanging on the hook.

Chief Dispatcher Frank Kergan called me on the phone and asked if I forgot that train order.

I said, "I did."

He called me in for an investigation and advised me I was entitled to have a representative. I told him I didn't need one as I had sure missed that order.

I told him the blunt truth and he accused me of trying to get fired. He then proceeded to tell me what I should say at the investigation and I did it his way. For this failure I served seventeen days without pay but was put back to work. Kergan was very pleasant to me and I always will remember his kindness. I don't think he wanted to fire me.

I was bumped out of Stampede by H. R. Denzene, which put me back on the extra list. I could have worked every day except they "sandwiched" the extra list jobs among the lower tail end of the list and that changed things.

I worked on the old Seattle Division all the time except in 1926, when I worked in the Relay Division between Seattle, Washington and St. Paul, Minnesota. I also worked in Spokane and liked working with the second trick chief, but they sent me on to work in Helena, Montana. The Wire Chief asked me if I knew why I was sent to Helena and I told him no. He told me about a telegrapher who wouldn't slow down for a check (when somebody opened the key to have him repeat something) and

46. Old coal dock at Lester. *Photo, Dallas Barnard.*

told me to go after him. For three days I made his life miserable until the Chief called me off.

Before coming to work on the Northern Pacific Railway, I worked as a commercial operator for the Old Postal in Portland, Oregon. My first job was as a telegraph-operator in 1917 in Bend, Oregon.

I still use my Western Union all capital letters typewriter that I bought from Jimmy Warren in 1943 while working as agent at Lester, Washington.

I was agent at Lester until 1946 and then bid in the agency at Sedro Woolley. Lester was quite a town and I got upset with the second trick operator who wouldn't pick up No. 5's mail at the post office. I got a dirty letter from the superintendent saying I was failing to superintend the operators under me. I wrote back and told him that Magee was doing this deliberately and that he fully knew his duties.

While I was agent at Lester, engineer Moon was on a troop train west of Cle Elum and he ran into a thirty-five miles per hour curve at about sixty miles per hour and was killed. They thought he forgot where he was. He wasn't a drinking man, so it had to be something else that made him do it. The fireman had to have his leg cut off to save his life as the engine was lying on his leg. Moon was a very likable man.

Thinking back to Lester, I remember Gorden Denier was the roundhouse foreman and Leo Ahearn was a machinist. The lever on my bug broke on the dot side and Ahearn repaired it by putting in a new lever. I still have that bug with me but the dot contact has been lost.

Otto Lemke was the third trick operator when I was there and he had trouble telegraphing. Magee bid in second trick Lester after another operator left, and he wanted to run things. I had to set him straight about who was boss. I remember the little store run by Mr. Hocking and the few things he sold to the town's people from shelves stocked with things from the past. I also remember the old railroad hotel where some of the crews stayed.

One day the second trick roundhouse foreman let a car of coal get away from him on the coal dock and it went down and

31

47. Coal car on coal dock at Lester. *Photo, Dallas Barnard.*

hit another car of coal. The foreman was so upset that he almost fainted.

I can't end this trip back in time without saying a little more about Jimmy Warren who was a very special person. He was a prince of a man in my estimation. During the '30s, there were hard times and I was out of work many times. Jimmy, would meet me on the streets of Auburn, Washington and ask me if I would be home about 3:00 p.m. I told him I would be home.

Then he'd say, "I'm going to be very sick about that time."

The railroad would call me to go to work and I'd get a day of work. I loved that man! He had heart and cared about people around him. Those days are gone now and all that remains are the memories.

85. NP depot and roundhouse at Lester, Washington. *Photo, Allen Miller collection.*

53. Billy Byrd, "The Poet of Steam." *Courtesy of Billy Byrd.*

RAIL TALES

I ALWAYS WANTED TO BE AN ENGINEER

By Billy Byrd - Madisonville, Kentucky

I was born May 28, 1922, in Adams, Tennessee. Adams is located on the Henderson Division of the Louisville and Nashville Railroad that is now CSX. From the time since I was big enough to know anything, I knew I wanted to be an engineer.

Everything was shipped by rail and there was a local train each way that unloaded freight everyday. I would slip off and go to the railroad and watch. I got several whippings about that. I introduced myself to the engineer, a kind, gracious gentleman named E.V. Partington. At first we talked, he on the engine and me on the ground. Then it was up in the cab. One day in 1931, I was nine years old and he gave me a ride. That settled it for good!

There is a heavy grade through Adams. I used to sit on the bank of the cut and watch the trains pull the grade. I would say to myself, 'One of these days, I'm going to make them do that.' -- and I did. I got aquainted with other engineers and they too let me ride with them. Every morning before school I would ride No. 53's engine until it met No. 52, then ride 52 back to Adams. Engineer Jimmy Long and Emil Speihs were on these jobs.

In the summertime I would ride the locals and the work trains. In 1937, the L&N put on a through non-stop train from Evansville to Nashville. Engineer Long was one of the engineers assigned to it. He came through Adams around 5:15 p.m. and he would throw a letter off to me. I really felt important that a man of Mr. Long's standing would pay attention to a boy like me.

He went north at 11:00 a.m. The school was in sight of the railroad and he would blow his whistle at me. I was the envy of the other kids. I graduated from school in May of 1941 and went to work for the railroad on, July 14, 1941. I was nineteen years old. I worked for a little while in the Maintenance of Way Department then transferred to Radnor Round House at Nashville, Tennessee. There I was with my beloved engines. I

35

started out as rod cup man greasing the side rods and other parts of the locomotives. Then it was my job to fill lubricators and finally running the turntable. Radnor Round House had thirty stalls, and with three divisions coming into Nashville, the Louisville, Evansville and Birmingham, it was a busy place. I finally graduated to Machinist Helper then outside Hostler Helper and <u>then</u> a job firing in the Nashville, Tennessee Terminal. The Nashville Terminal was a company unto itself but was jointly owned by the Louisville and Nashville and the Nashville, Chattanooga & St. Louis Railroad -- always referred to as the N&C.

I thought my firing career was going to be over before it got started. I was firing for engineer Frank Baker who was an engineer of the old school. The N.C.& St. L. bought some new 4-8-4 type engines called "yellow jackets" by the engine crews because of their yellow color and semi-streamlining. They were running a test train with two of the yellow jackets double heading with 100 cars. (The first 100 car train I had ever seen.)

Nashville is located on a hillside and our job was to help the test train out of town. We were coupled onto the caboose with one of the 300 series 2-8-0 engines. Nashville had a big anti-smoke campaign on and you were written up for making hardly any smoke at all.

Mr. Baker said, "Boy, I've got to have the putty now to get this man out of here."

I said. "What about the smoke?"

He said, "<u>I'll</u> take care of the smoke!"

He was trimming that old engine pretty good, shoring on that train. I would bust the bottom of that scoop against the fire door liner to see just how much I could make. When we went by Union Station it looked like the Navy had laid a smoke screen.

After we had gotten the fellows out of town, we came back and spotted by the yard office just across from the train shed. A well dressed fellow climbed up on the engine and stood around not saying anything. Mr. Baker who was about six feet four inches tall, could hide behind a wheat straw and if he drank a strawberry pop, could look like a thermometer. He was nicknamed Shorty. Shorty asked him his business. He was the city of Nashville Smoke Inspector. He gave me a ticket for making black smoke and gave Mr. Baker one for allowing me to do it.

Shorty said, "What do you want us to do with these things?"

The inspector said, "Take them down to Judge Doyle in the morning at 9:00 a.m. He'll know what to do with them."

Mr. Baker said, "Fireboy, give me your ticket."

I did, and he got off of his seat, put his foot on the fire door pedal, the door opened and he threw them into the firebox.

He said, " There they go."

Well, the inspector didn't know what to say so he just stood there. Mr. Baker asked him if he had a permit to ride the engine.

He said, "No."

Mr. Baker then told him if he wanted to ride to go see the Superintendent and get a permit, then come back and ride all he wanted to.

But until he got it, "BY GOD get off and stay off!"

The inspector never said a word, but got off and slunk down through the train shed like a dog with his tail between his legs.

I said, "We're fired, we're fired, we haven't got a sign of a job. They won't even have an investigation."

The old man said, "To hell with 'em, I'm sixty-five."

I said, "But I'm not!"

To my knowledge he never heard anything about it.

Another time I was firing for him and the company had put smoke consumers on the engines that consisted of steam jets on the sides of the firebox. The steam would blow over the top of the fire and hold the smoke down where it was supposed to burn. Company instructions were to keep it on at all times.

I had them checked, just cracked open so if anyone came around I could testify to that fact. Mr. Baker was oiling around on my side. He looked up.

"Boy! have you got them damn smoke burners on?"

I said, "Yes sir."

He said, "Turn them damn things off. All they're fit for is to make a hellava racket. Clinker the fire and use all the coal and water in the country."

I agreed.

He said, " Now I'll tell you what we will do."

About that time Mr. Walter Moore, the Traveling Engineer, came around the corner of the tender and was hearing every word. Mr. Moore was a fine man and he had a glass eye. I'm trying to signal to Shorty that Mr. Moore was there but Shorty paid no attention.

He said, "You watch on your side and I'll watch on my side and if we see Old Tangle Eye Moore coming, we will jerk them on real quick."

Mr. Moore just shook his head and walked off toward the Kayne Avenue Roundhouse.

I said, "Look yonder, Mr. Baker, what you just done."

He said, "I'll be damned, you can't even talk about 'em that they're not trying to listen to what you're saying."

These Nashville Terminal fellows were a fine bunch to work with but I liked road work much better, so I transferred to the Henderson Sub-Division of the Evansville Division. On my first trip I wondered what I had gotten into. I had known the engineer, Felix Crouch, since I was twelve years old. I really felt big throwing that clothes box up on that big 2-8-2 Mikado engine.

Felix got on the engine and said, "Can you keep her hot?"

I said, "I think I can."

He said, "Hell, Boy, there ain't no think to it. If you can't do it, here is where to get off. Here is where friendship ends."

We left and about twenty-five miles out of Evansville the stoker quit. I grabbed the scoop and started firing by hand and he was working the stoker trying to get the obstruction out, which he did. We got about halfway to Nashville when I looked in the firebox. It looked like the Rocky Mountains, I've never seen such a mess. I wanted to clean the fire.

He said, "We are halfway, she will be okay."

I doubted it as we hadn't hit the hilly part of the railroad.

RAIL TALES

We were starting on the hill through my old home town when she started failing for steam. I couldn't get any smoke out of her. I thought, *'Oh, Lord, please don't let me have to blow up steam in my home town on my first trip.'* I couldn't keep coal in the back end of the firebox. I shut the stoker jets clean off. I told Felix I'd done all I could do, did he have any suggestions?

He said, "Turn the squirt hose on and run the water in the stoker conveyor trough."

I thought he'd lost what little he had. Whoever heard of firing an engine on water, but I'm not doing any good, so I'll do what he says.

The stack started blacking up, the steam gauge hand started climbing, and when we went through Adams she was setting right on the pop. What had happened was when I was firing by hand, I had gotten the fire heavier in front and the exhaust was tearing the fire where there was the least resistance. The dry coal wasn't heavy enough to stay on the firebed where the wet coal was.

As the years went by I was promoted. I never cared for the diesels but I took them and did the best I could with them. But something was always missing.

A lot of funny things happened and there was something different every day. I was engineer on a work train and it was bitterly cold with snow on the ground. We were picking up scrap. Most Maintenance of Way workmen were black. They could take a piece of wet broomsedge and get a fire going in seconds, whereas I couldn't have started one with a barrel of diesel fuel. It was in February and bitterly cold, and those two old fellows were arguing about the weather.

One of them said, "Old groundhog caused this weather, that's what done it. That old groundhog."

The other said, " Huh uh, brother, you don't know what yo're talking about, this is the Lawd's work. He ain't turning his business over to no groundhog."

Another time I was coming out of Nashville with an empty hopper train. I had two old six-axle Alcos that took an iron worker to get on and off of them. The cab doors were so narrow a big man had trouble getting through them. I'm a fairly large fellow and I would have to turn sideways and "suck up my gut" when I had to go through. Leaving Nashville the head engine quit loading. I did all I knew to do and couldn't get it to work. I called the yardmaster and told him to send an electrician to see if he could fix it. Two came and they fooled around with it for about an hour.

I said, " I see that you don't know anymore about it than I do. I'm going to ask the yardmaster if I can bring this crippled engine back and leave it so they can work on it. I can handle the train with one engine."

They said, "Let us try one more thing."

Now the brakeman was a great big man. I don't see how he could get in the door at all. It was dark and raining. One of the electricians had a screwdriver about three feet long. He stuck it in that control cabinet and I never heard a 155 cannon in World War II make such a racket, and a stream of fire shot across the cab. When the dust settled there was no brakeman to be found. How he got through that door without killing himself I'll never know.

After we had our laugh, I started looking for him. There he stood in the middle of the track in the rain, in the glare of the headlight.

I told him, "No harm done, come on back in here."

He did and I asked him, "Why did you run?"

He said, "I thought there ought to be somebody left to tell them what happened."

So we had another laugh.

One more story I remember should have the title, "Sonny, Don't Leave Me." We had this fellow named Wilson Teague who was making his first trip flagging. They had a real long train, no radios and were operating under train orders. They had to take a certain siding, and when in the clear, close the switch behind them. It was just the reverse heading out on the main. The engineer was pulling out at a pretty good gait. He thought he was running slow enough for the flagman to get the switch and then get on.

The conductor told Teague that he would get the switch as he thought they were going too fast for him to get it. He didn't want to put the air on him as they would have to get a signal to the head end to get started again. Teague was standing on the back end of the caboose, and as it happened the conductor couldn't get on.

He hollared to Teague, "Sonny, don't leave me!" meaning for him to ease the air on and stop the train.

Teague said, "By God, I'll stay with you."

He ran back to the caboose and got his lunch bucket and jumped off. Consequently, they both got left. There was a telephone at the switch, so the conductor called thtrain dispatcher and told him what had happened. The dispatcher had the operator at the next station hold the train order board red. When the engineer stopped he was advised that he had run off and left his conductor and rear brakeman. He had to cut his engine off and go back and get them.

From then on if you saw Brother Teague and you said, "Sonny, don't leave me," there had better be some distance between the two of you.

I worked from July 14, 1941, to July 14, 1984. In 1977, I went to the Folk Festival at Washington, DC to represent the engineers and railroads. In 1983, Charles Kuralt of "On the Road" spent three days riding the engine with me. On my last trip I was stopped at Hopkinsville, Kentucky by about fifty people. The mayor gave me the key to the city and made me Honorary Mayor. I was the second man in the history of the town to get this honor. The mayor of Adams, my home town, proclaimed Billy Byrd Day. The mayor of Madisonville made me official Ambassador for the town. I received a nice personal letter from the president of the railroad, thanking me for the many friends I had made for the company during the years, waving from the cab, etc.

I have a cupola caboose in my backyard. I also have two steam tractors, a sixteen-sixty horse power double cylinder full size Nichols & Shepard and a 1/2 size sixty-five horse power Case.

RAIL TALES

After I retired and up until this year, I ran the engine regularly at the Tennessee Valley Railroad Museum at Chattanooga and plan to do some more this coming summer.

My identification number is 313367. Seniority date was July 14, 1941, and retired July 14, 1984.

A FAVOR

By Don Shane - Tacoma, Washington

One of the fondest *memories in my thirty-five years of railroading took place on the third day of service on the Northern Pacific Railway. My first day was April 15, 1947, and I was working second trick telegrapher's job in Ravensdale, Washington.

I arrived in this small mining town located along the main line of the Northern Pacific, on my Harley Davidson motorcycle the day before to break in, then work April 15 and 16. April 17 was my birthday and it must have been my day off, because I planned on going to my folk's house in Bremerton. (Mom always made a big fuss about my birthday.)

Anyhow, when I woke up, it was raining cats and dogs and when I went over to the boarding house for breakfast I must have had a sad look on my face. Ruth Trueblood, who worked third trick was in the boarding house and asked me what was the matter. I told her I couldn't go home for my birthday because it was raining. She looked at me for a minute and then she offered to lend me her car.

Then I had to admit I didn't have enough money for the ferry boat to Bremerton and for gasoline. To make a long story short, I left Ravensdale with Ruth's Model A Ford, plus her change purse full of money. I went to Bremerton, had a good time and returned to Ravensdale with a heart full of thanks for a wonderful, trusting soul, named Ruth Trueblood. I retired as assistant Chief Dispatcher on the Burlington Northern Railroad in Seattle on January 31, 1983.

When I asked Don for a story, he grinned and said he thought he had one. Then he made me promise to use it, if he wrote it.   Ruth Eckes

RAIL TALES

A SPECIAL AGENT'S MEMORIES
By Jerry Pratt - Milton, Washington

I come from a railroad family. My grandfather David Boyes, on my father's side, was a telegrapher and taught my uncle Ed Boyes, to telegraph. Ed was a telegrapher in Libby, Montana on the Great Northern Railway in 1911.

Law enforcement started with my father, William Henry Pratt, when he was the Chief of Police in Libby, Montana. While working as chief, he heard there was a job available as Special Agent on the Great Northern. He applied and got the job in Spokane, Washington in 1919.

I was two years old when we moved to Spokane. He worked for quite a while on the Great Northern and when they wanted to promote him to a job in Havre, Montana, he told them no. Then he got a job for the Spokane Police Department and stayed there twentyfive years.

I always liked railroading and after I was grown in 1942, my Uncle Hugh Boyes in Tacoma called me to come and he would get me a job. He worked on the Northern Pacific Railway as a Special Agent. By this time I was married and had one son. I first went to Seattle to talk to the boss, John Winquist, who was the head Special Agent.

He looked me over and said, "Yeah, you're big enough, but you'll have to take a physical."

I took the physical and they discovered I was color blind. I told the doctor I wouldn't be running trains or switching cars and that I just wanted a job in the Special Agent Department. He said "In that case we can take you."

I started work in Seattle on August 1, 1942, and worked for three months. The department became short handed in Tacoma, so I went there to work and stayed with my uncle until I brought my family over from Seattle. During this time, I had to fill in as a shop watchman and patrolman, both downtown in Tacoma and in South Tacoma and this continued for a while. I

31. Great Northern station at Libby, Montana. L to R: Lee Ketchum, Clerk; Ed Boyes, Telegrapher; J.D. Hunter, Agent. Picture taken in 1911. *Jerry Pratt collection.*

remember the same situation between the big Union Depot and in the old Service Building.

Thinking back to those days, I remember Worthington Smith, Superintendent on the Tacoma Division, and a little happening.

It was on Sunday morning and the old Service Building housed the Pullman Company, electricians and special agents in this big, long building along Track 5. Somehow, the building caught fire and by the time I got there it was really enveloped in flames.

Ol' Worthington showed up and when he came up to me he said, "Jerry, who the hell was the dumb S.O.B. that turned in the alarm?"

I don't think he thought the building worth saving and I'll never forget that incident.

Worth is now dead. He retired and went down to La Jolla, Caifornia, I remember asking him what he was going to do down there.

He said, "I'm going to buy a place with a bunch of orange trees on it and I'm going to inject them with vodka and have instant screw drivers."

About 1964, I was at the Kelso depot and a phone call came in. Jack Flagg was the agent at Kelso and hc said LeRoy Beeler, a Northern Pacific conductor wanted me on the phone. Beeler had a brand new caboose and it was on a track where the Longview, Portland and Northern Railroad came into Longview Junction. The crew on the LP&N stole all the cushions from that new caboose and Beeler was HOT! I drove my car down to Longview Junction and spotted the LP&N engine.

I didn't hesitate a minute and climbed up into the engine and said, "I'll tell you what I'm going to do. You take those cushions and put them back into that caboose over there, and then I'm going to see the General Manager of the LP&N."

That was all it took. I could have charged them with theft but I didn't.

A special agent's job could be difficult and grisly as well as dangerous. One afternoon in the Tacoma Yard. I was talking to a switchman named Wasalewski. He was going to couple some cars together just as a switcher engineer kicked some cars down the track. He stepped right between two cars and was cut in half before my eyes.

Another time, there was a Signal Department truck driver up at Bellingham, Washington who had an accident on Thanksgiving day and was killed. They called his boss to go over and tell his widow the news. He wouldn't go, so they called everybody they could to do this job and couldn't get anybody. They called me in the middle of my Thanksgiving Day dinner and I drove over to Gig Harbor to break the news.

I finally found the place and said to her, "I have some bad news for you."

She invited me in and I told her what had happened.

She sat for a minute and then said, "Would you have a bottle of beer?"

I did this job twice for the signal department over the years and those are things I would like to forget.

Once in a while a little human nature story would surface and a laugh eased some of the bad times. The Union Depot in Tacoma was heated by a central plant over on Dock Street and all the controls were in Jim Howe's office.

The women working in the depot would come up to Dave and say, "Mr. Howe, it's awful cold down here and we've got to have some heat."

Dave would tell them, "Okay girls, I'll take care of it."

So, in about thirty minutes he'd go down to see them and say, "How's everything now girls?"

They would always tell him fine. He used to chuckle over this, as he never did a thing about turning up the heat.

Another time there was a hobo on crutches right near the River Street bridge. A train started to pull out of town and he got up on these crutches, waiting for an empty box car. I was standing close by and warned him that he was going to get killed trying to get on. He ignored me and after throwing his crutches into the box car, he leaped into it in a second.

Looking back at me he yelled, "Never try to help a cripple!"

These are some of the things that stick in my memory of years gone by. Those years went by like a brisk wind and I retired June 1, 1977.

HOW A NICKNAME WAS BORN
By Blackie Moser - Auburn, Washington

Nicknames are part of railroading too. A Northern Pacific engineer I remember from the past was H.D. Wolters and the nickname he acquired matched his initials.

One day when he was leaving Lester on a mallet helper, he went up on the running board and walked out around and up onto the top of the engine to get one of the turret valves to open, in order to get steam to the dynamo.

He stood up just in time to get the bridge girder along side his head, and it carried him over the top of the engine cab. He slid off along side the tender, onto the right-of-way, and when the caboose came along, he swung up on the caboose.

The blow to his head didn't even knock him out, but he had the imprint of the rivits all down the side of his head. Anybody else would have been killed under these circumstances.

Railroaders always quick to see humor, dubbed him "Hard Dome" and that was the only name he was known by from then on.

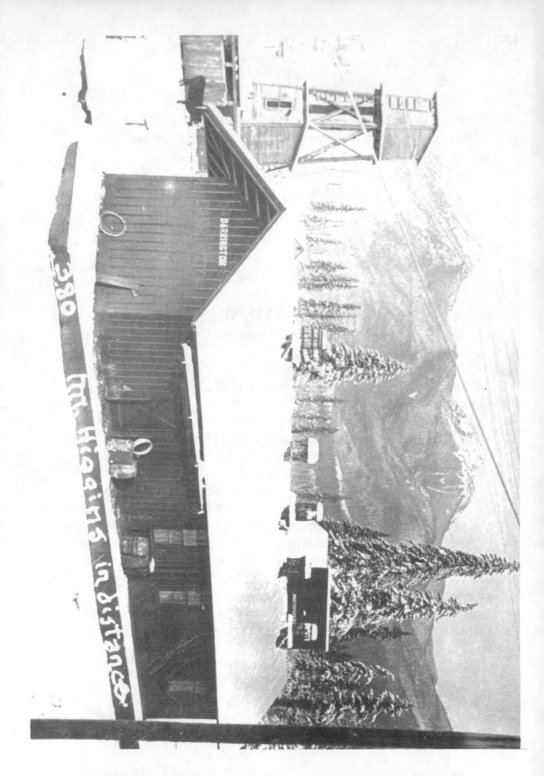

4. NP depot at Darrington, Washington *J. M Fredrickson Collection*

48

DARRINGTON IN 1927
By Tom Strand - Auburn, Washington

About 1927, my father was working on a Northern Pacific Railway switch job that worked exclusively in Darrington, Washington. Darrington was a little mining and timber town located eighty miles from Seattle, fifty miles from Everett and thirty miles from Arlington, the closest town of any size. All around it, except to the west of town are mountains. Whitehorse (elevation 6,852 feet) is the most prominent. It is always snow-capped year round and dominates the town.

The first Northern Pacific train chugged into the town of Darrington on July 1, 1901 and its arrival was an exciting event for that community. The daily arrival of the train was the occasion for everyone in town to drop whatever he or she was doing and head for the depot to see who was arriving. The train also brought supplies and mail sacks.

The train made one trip a day for years, with the crew staying overnight in Darrington and returning the next morning to Arlington. Later it made a round trip daily and still later a night trip was added. Passenger service had long been discontinued and in 1967 the depot that stood between Railroad Avenue and Montague Avenue at Darrington Street was burned down by the Darrington Fire Department.

A majority of the southerners in Darrington are "Tarheels," natives of North Carolina, but some hail from Georgia and Tennessee. About 1912, they began trickling into Darrington. Between the loggers and the miners the town was considered to be "wild and woolly."

The Northern Pacific Railway had a caboose tied up on a spur that was not in use at the time. I remember dad asked our mother, my brother and me to come up to Darrington for the summer and stay in the caboose. We caught the (Galloping Goose) Budd Car that ran each day to Bellingham from Seattle. We got off at Everett and got on the mixed train (freight and

5. Gas-Electric car used on the Darrington Branch. *Warren Wing Collection*

32. NP Conductor Tom Strand working at his caboose desk.

passenger) that went from Everett to Darrington each day. I remember that Claude Rogers was the conductor and an engineer named Aerie Marion were on the mixed train crew. I don't recall the brakemen.

After we got on the Darrington Branch, Conductor Claude Rogers cut willow switches for my brother and me, then opened the windows so we could hit the ferns and flowers as the train puffed along. When we got to Darrington we moved into the caboose. I have many wonderful memories of hiking and swimming. We also had strict orders and warnings to stay on established trails as there were many bootleg stills in the area and the natives didn't like strangers in their midst.

One day my brother and I walked up the tracks past the depot which was the main line of the Sauk River Timber Company. We were about a quarter of a mile up the tracks when a boy about twelve years old with a .22 rifle stopped us, and ordered us to dance for about fifteen minutes while he held his gun on us. We were afraid to disobey him because we thought he would shoot us.

All this while his mother was sitting on the front porch of a house nearby, smoking a pipe and watching this scene. We began to cry (we were only about six or seven years old). The more we cried the harder he made us dance. Finally the old lady on the porch said we must have learned our lesson about straying too far from home and the boy lowered his gun and we ran. This experience was a story told in our family for many years.

MEMORIES OF THE ROCKY MOUNTAIN DIVISION

By Olive Middleton - Townsend, Montana

It's been twenty-five years since I retired from the Rocky Mountain Division of the Northern Pacific Railway. I hired out in the years of the Second World War and many men went to war leaving the railroad short on personnel. They were forced to hire girls to man their stations and that is how I happened to go to work as a telegrapher, even though I never went to telegraph school to learn Morse Code.

My husband Lyall was a CTC (Centralized Taffic Control) maintainer. We had no children and when he found out I wanted to go to work, he asked me if I would be interested in his job. He rode the rails in a motorcar and I declined that.

Agent Vanderberg's wife in our home town of Toston and I wanted to learn how to telegraph, so he offered to get us some supplies and get us both started. We began that fall of 1942 and trained all winter, until after the first of the year. The chief dispatcher in Missoula contacted him and asked if he had any operators ready to go to work. Well, we were not ready. I had too many things going for me — bridge club, Ladies Aid, church, etc. Mr. Vanderberg asked me if I wanted to learn station work in the office. I said yes, and went over to the depot every day for six weeks or so, learning all I could about running a station. My formal education had only been through the eighth grade.

The Missoula chief dispatcher again contacted Vanderberg mid-summer, to see if I was ready to go to work. I went to Missoula, passed the examination and went to work that same day, July, 1943. I was forty-one years old.

I spent two years on the line, working as relief agent. Then my home town of Toston came up for bid, and I was able to bid it in. I worked for four companies: the Northern Pacific Railway, the Northern Pacific Transport, Railway Express and the Western Union Telegraph Company. I sent out four sets of reports every month, made requisitions for supplies and remitted all money to the different companies.

Olive Middleton

RAIL TALES

Each morning at 8:00 a.m. I copied a lineup from the dispatcher to give to the signal maintainer and section men who had work to do along the tracks. Then I got a thirty minute break to go check the yard for any cars ordered for shipping. I had one hour off for lunch and my work hours were 8:00 a.m. to 5:00 p.m.

When the passenger train arrived daily, I had to work it. The farmers brought in cream to ship. We had a platform truck and the farmers would set the cans on the truck, so I could more easily lift the cans to load on the train. At this station the farmers and miners shipped grain, hay, ore, livestock and spuds in cars.

The dispatcher gave us train orders for some of the trains traveling through there. The first hoops were made of a single length of a branch. The small end was curled back and fastened with a wire spring, which held the orders and we handed them up while the train was moving through town.

The second hoop was made of a length of wood with two extensions at the end and resembled a big "Y." We tied string with double slip knots, which held the orders and attached it to the "V" end of the rod.

Some years later there was another invention that made handing up orders much easier and safer for the operators. There was a frame on the platform that we fitted the long end of the "Y" shaped hoop into, and the engine and train crews could snag the strings right out of the open end of the "Y" where the orders were strung. It was called a hoop stand. The train crews occasionally missed getting their orders and had to back the train up to get them.

For the most part the trainmen didn't get upset over it but there was one named Murphy who was "mad" and showed he was upset. One day I got even with him though when he came down the main track, when actually he should have been in the siding. I flagged him down and angrily stamped around, indicating for him to get in the siding . . . which he did!

One day, a young brakeman on the local freight made a remark about how the blouse I was wearing fit me, as he was going by on the train. I quickly came back at him with, "It's all

55

mine!" It never happened again. All the trainmen and others who did business with me were very respectful.

Thinking back to those days, there weren't many girls working on the railroad as telegraphers when I went to work. It was a good job and I enjoyed every minute of it. I was born in 1902 and am ninety-one years old. I can remember those years as if they were yesterday.

58. James R. Hudon, Telegrapher. *Photo: Ed Eckes.*

RAIL TALES

LEVERMAN ON THE CHICAGO & NORTH WESTERN

By James R. Hudon -- Federal Way, Washington

Sometime in 1939, while working as an extra board telegrapher-clerk-leverman for the Chicago & North Western Railroad in Milwaukee, Wisconsin, I worked the third trick at the Kinnickkinnik River Bridge Tower Electric Plant. It also powered swinging the bridge that was only a few feet above the river. The bridge had to be opened to allow boats of the fishing fleet to pass.

One night before going to work I was suffering from a terrific pain in the palm of my right hand, the first time I had experienced such an affliction. I dropped by a drug store and told the pharmacist my problem. He prepared a mixture and I drank it. I didn't tell him that I was on my way to work. On the job a short time later I was awakened by a switchman who had to climb the ladder to the tower on top of the bridge to wake me up. He probably thought I had been drinking but I assured him that I was able to work. Then, thinking a little, I realized that my falling asleep was the result of the mixture given to me at the drug store. I finished the trick without further incident, but I never forgot that experience!

I also remember sometime in 1939, when I worked third trick on another tower-bridge job over the Kinnikkinnik River. The power to swing the bridge was a Fairbanks-Morse engine and it was started by compressed air in a tank charged by an electric motor. I swung the bridge open about daylight to allow the fishing fleet to pass. These fishing boats didn't start at the same time, so I kept the bridge open, since no rail traffic was due. After I figured the last boat had passed, I tried to start the engine, but no luck. I kept charging the compressed air tank but the engine would not start when the air released. I phoned for the signal maintainer and when he arrived at the shore, he had to oar the company boat to the bridge, and climb the piling to get to the bridge. He wasn't able to start the engine either and I was happy about that, because a new man was usually "suspect" when problems arose. He oared me to shore in the company boat and picked up the first trick leverman and took him over to the bridge. Later that day I met the signal maintainer and he said the bar connected to the engine wheel did not travel close enough to make contact that should have energized the engine. Those were problems that could cause major delays until repaired and big headaches for personnel.

MALTBY HILL

By Bob Heirman - Snohomish, Washington

I was runnin' in the Bayside Yard on a night so clear
And my mind wandered back to yesteryear.
I could see the hogger on his seat box like a king upon a throne,
Never mind the fact that forty years had flown.
I could see the water bobbin' in the water glass,
I could see the gauges lit up and all the shiny brass.
His hand was on the throttle and a kerchief 'round his neck
And me a bailin' coal on the swaying deck.
'Though I was in the Bayside Yard on this night so still,
My mind was back in yesteryear a battlin' Maltby Hill.

1. Maltby local, north of Woodinville in 1941. *Bob Heirman Collection.*

8. NP hostler, Warren Graybeal servicing Challenger engine 5138 at Easton, Washington during the 1940's. *Photo, J.M. Fredrickson.*

RAIL TALES

EASTON, WASHINGTON - 1942
By Warren Graybeal - Shawnee, Oklahoma

It all started back in 1942 at the small village of Easton, Washington, located along the main line of the Northern Pacific Railway on the Tacoma Division. The Japanese had bombed Pearl Harbor on December 7, 1941, plunging us into a global conflict that was to last until August of 1945. I had just completed my junior year in high school and had gone to Oregon where I worked on farms during the hay and wheat season. I was on a wheat ranch out of Durfur, Oregon when I received a telegram to come home at once, no explanation, just come home at once. Upon arriving home Dad, who worked in the roundhouse at Easton, informed me they needed a grease monkey and George Pilgrim said I could have the job. Well, this created a small problem since this was July, 1942 and I wouldn't be seventeen until August, which was the legal age requirement to go to work. George put me to work and held up the paper work for two weeks.

Then he said, "They would have to pay you anyway."

Since this little arrangement worked out all right, I was a full fledged grease monkey at the Easton roundhouse.

At this stage of the war, men were being taken in the draft so fast that the available manpower was getting pretty scarce. This was the reason that at one time there were as many as five high school boys working in the roundhouse. Some of us who were involved in sports had to have the older men double-over for us, since we worked seven days a week. At one time I owed fifty-six hours to other men which had to be paid back. This was our only way for time off since there was no extra-board to fill the vacancy to give a day off. Of course, the older men liked this situation with us kids because it gave them a day off when they needed it.

Easton at this time was a pretty busy place. It was the end of the double track eastbound and helper station westbound for Stampede Pass. We had six passenger engines a day plus extra sections carrying troops, as well as all the freight traffic. We usually had six or seven of the old Z3 class Mallets, W1 class

61

9. NP Easton depot. Picture taken in 1944. *Photo, J.M. Fredrickson.*

(Crab) as passenger helper, and once in a while a W3 class (Mike) on hand. In the winter time we had rotaries and spreaders on hand to keep the line open with the heavy snow that used to fall across the Cascades. There were six engine crews and three pilots working out of Easton most of the time. I can remember engineers such as George Hogan, Jim Loasby, H.D. Wolters, and Nimitz, who we called, "Drawbar Nimitz" after the day he thought the head end was shut off and he was on the rear helper behind the caboose. When he shut off the bottom bolts in the caboose, the drawbar let loose causing it to raise up and come uncoupled. This in turn pulled the air, which set the train into emergency stop. The train was stopping faster than Nimitz could stop the old Z3. They were right in front of the depot when this happened and never did a conductor and brakeman leave a caboose so fast!

Names of firemen who cross my mind are Bill Sorenson, Jim Colson, and Ray Ashley. These firemen were pretty much regulars at Easton, others came and went. Most of the engineers stayed in helper service at Easton as regulars. We had three pilots, Bobby Bartro comes to mind.

There was a full compliment of operators, and agent Roy Spaulding. Operators came and went pretty regular at that time. I recall Harlan Plith and Norm Peterson as two of the many who worked at Easton depot.

If memory serves me right, I was a grease monkey for only about a month when I was made fire cleaner. Well, the first one I cleaned was an old Mallet, as we called them, and I shook her down good. So well in fact, there was no fire left. There was nothing to do but head for the woodpile we kept handy for such goofy mistakes and get some waste, soak it with fortnight oil and build a new fire. I didn't make that mistake again. I was a little less vigorous on the shaker bar after that.

We had machinists and helpers in the roundhouse at this time. Vern Raver and Stan Hages were machinists, and I remember Orten Allen as one of the helpers. Stan Hages was working the day one of the Z6 Challengers decided to leave the roundhouse on its own. It ran all the switches east of the roundhouse and headed down the helper track for the main line.

Our west bound passenger No. 5 was due before long. The safety feature of a derail before going on to the main line saved the day. When it hit the derail it left the track, tore up about 150 feet of roadbed and buried into the dirt almost to the point of laying over on its side. Since it remained upright a crane was brought in the next day and by the day after they had it back on the rails. After that little experience, orders were issued that whenever a Z6 or Z8 was parked in the roundhouse, they were to have three big chains under the drive wheels on each side, and air from the roundhouse compressor hooked up to the engine at all times. No more runaways!

It was our job to see that helper engines were set out in time for the crews to check out the equipment and get to the east end of the yard to await hookup to westbound freights. Passenger helpers sat on a small side track west of the depot so they could hook onto the head end of these trains. One day helper engineer Alex Taylor hooked onto the head end of No.5. After we had checked the ash pans, filled the water tank on the Q6 main line engine, and all the express and mail was unloaded, the highball was given and out of town they went. There were two helper engines coming down the wrong way, which they did sometimes if the east bound tracks were tied up. Both engineers (the engineer on No. 5's engine and the engineer on the helper engine) had a wait order telling them to wait at Easton until the helpers were in the clear. The operator at the time tried to flag from the rear, but no one looked back or saw him. Alex was reading his orders when he met the helpers in a head-on crash. Luckily, no one was hurt, but Alex got time off.

It was our job to call all the crews and many a time during that winter of 1942 we were wading snow four feet deep to get some of them called. After getting back on a warm engine your overall legs would be wet from the melting snow and when you were off the engine they would freeze stiff.

The roundhouse crew was complimented by regular firemen who came to Easton as hostlers on bid. Usually their stay was short because they could make more money on a switching or main line job whenever they were able to hold one. I remember some of them, such as Jerry Brown, who let me borrow his car to go on senior sneak just before graduation. Also Bob Ballard, who I was working with the night that Gene Pellini, a section hand, was smothered in the coal dock. We had two Z3 engines at the coal dock to coal up when the call buzzer sounded at the depot. Bob told me to go get the call while he went ahead with the coaling. When I got back, he had pulled up the rear engine and when he opened the coal chute, Gene came out! The coal had been freezing in the dock, so he had been put in there to break the coal loose in order that we could coal the engines. He was supposed to wear a safety rope, but didn't. Evidently the coal gave way under him and slid in on top, suffocating him. Anyway, that was a sad time and it was pretty hard to get our work done during the rest of the night.

Another hostler was Sam Watterson and for some reason, we worked very well together. We each did whatever job came up — moving equipment, cleaning fires, or whatever. Sam and I could get our work done and spend more time at Ed's Cafe than any other crew. Now, I don't think Sam and I broke any rules; we might have bent them a little. Like the time there was a freight stalled down below the crossing, I have forgotten why, but they were trying to get pulled up without helpers on and couldn't make it. Sam and I were on an old Mallet, and Sam suggested we give them a pull. I thought that was a good idea, so I got back on the tank step so I could hook and unhook while Sam played engineer. We got them rolling, I pulled the pin and gave Sam a highball so he could get up to the next switch and I could jump off and throw the switch back in time for them to go by. Needless to say, I had the switch unlocked before we ever started our little maneuver. George Pilgrim took a very dim view of our helping hand.

When the Z6s and Z8s started running into Easton, they had to be taken onto the main line west of town, and turned on the wye. These engines were too large to go over the mountain. They slipped on the tight curves, and there were only six inches of clearance on each side in the Stampede Tunnel. One was taken through the tunnel, and the crew nearly roasted, so that was the end of that.

Anyway, I was advanced to hostler helper by the time Sam was there. One day we had a Z6 to turn, so we dropped down over the rubber switch at the east end.

Sam said, "Shall we see what she can do?"

I said, "Let her go."

Well, we emptied the depot when we went by and when we got to the west end of the wye, Sam was grabbing everything in the cab trying to get stopped.

We got her shut down by the Easton Dam and Sam said, "By God, I thought we were going to Seattle there for a little bit."

George took a dim view of that little episode also.

One day on first trick, just after 7:00 a.m., we noticed a bunch of hoboes sleeping in the old roundhouse. It was pretty cold out, so Sam and I decided we would warm them up next time we went by with an engine. When next time came, we opened up the blow-off cock on the boiler, and filled the old roundhouse with steam and water. That sure emptied out the place in a hurry!

Another time we had two engines at the coal dock so we uncoupled and I put coal on the rear one and Sam was handling the front. I moved on down to the cinder pit and stopped to check the fire. I decided I needed to shake it down a little. I'd just gotten down out of the cab to check the ash pan, when I looked up and here came Sam. I couldn't get to the whistle in time. I was trying to flag him down but he was leaning out the cab waving at someone going up the tracks. I guess he finally caught a glimpse of me out of the corner of his eye because to this day I can see his head popping in and out of that cab.

The engines hit so hard it rang both bells. Sam said he grabbed everything in that cab, even put it in forward motion to try and get stopped. He didn't expect me to stop as he thought I had gone on to the roundhouse. Again George Pilgrim gave us a lecture.

One day a Z6 that had been down in the Yakima canyon came in with horse all over the front of the engine. During Vern Ravers's checkup underneath the engine, he found the horse's head wedged up in the running gear and they had to get under there with crowbars and pry it out.

Another of their jobs involved getting into the firebox of a Z6 or Z8 after we shook out the fire so they could replace a section of burned out grate. Arch brick were always falling out of the top of the firebox. These would catch in the grates out on the road when the firemen tried to shake the fire down and would hold them open. This allowed the fire to burn under the grates and the heat caused them to burn up. You could only stay in the firebox about five minutes because it was so hot. I helped them one time and that was enough for me.

All of these things happened in 1942, at the town of Easton, Washington on the old Northern Pacific Railway. Those were the days of the old steam engines, the old freight hogs, the forty hundreds, the huge Challengers, the Mikes, the little switchers, the Q6, and the long sleek A engines, such as the 2626 which worked the North Coast Limited. Those were the days before diesels took over and progress changed the face of railroading forever. Easton, Martin, Stampede, Lester, Eagle Gorge, and so on down the list, no longer exist as railroad points. Many of the people I have mentioned have gone on, but some are still with us. Memories of the old Easton Yard and the people who worked there are good memories, and I am glad to share them.

3. No. 43 supplying steam to the F.H. Hogue Frozen Food Packing Plant while the plant boiler was under repairs. *Photo, Al Farrow*

RAIL TALES

NUMBER 43 AS A STATIONARY AT KENT
By Al Farrow - Auburn, Washington

At the height of the pea harvest in Kent, Washington in July 1938, the packing house steam boiler failed. The steam was necessary to blanch the peas at the F. H. Hogue frozen food processing plant.

The Northern Pacific Railway came to the rescue by furnishing a locomotive to supply steam. The Number 43, 2-8-0, Y class, was sent from Auburn to act as a stationary boiler. At that point in time Frank Possolo and I were cut off the firemen's active list and were working in the roundhouse in Auburn. We were sent to Kent to act as stationary firemen. We worked around the clock, eight hours on and eight hours off, relieving each other.

After the engine was spotted and hooked up to the steam line, they opened the steam valve and all hell broke loose. The plant boiler had been set to furnish 100 pounds of steam and the locomotive was putting out 200 pounds. It just about blew up their equipment. After bringing the pressure down to 100 pounds, everything was going well. After a couple of days the engine stopped steaming. No amount of grate shaking and using the blower would make the fire burn.

The roundhouse in Auburn sent a boilermaker to trouble shoot. He opened up the front end and cleaned the spark arresting screens and that solved the problem.

Because the engine hadn't been moved, the steam exhaust didn't clean out the front end, hence the front end plugged up. After that we regularly scraped the screens with a special tool and had no more trouble. We continued on the job until the frozen food plant boiler was repaired.

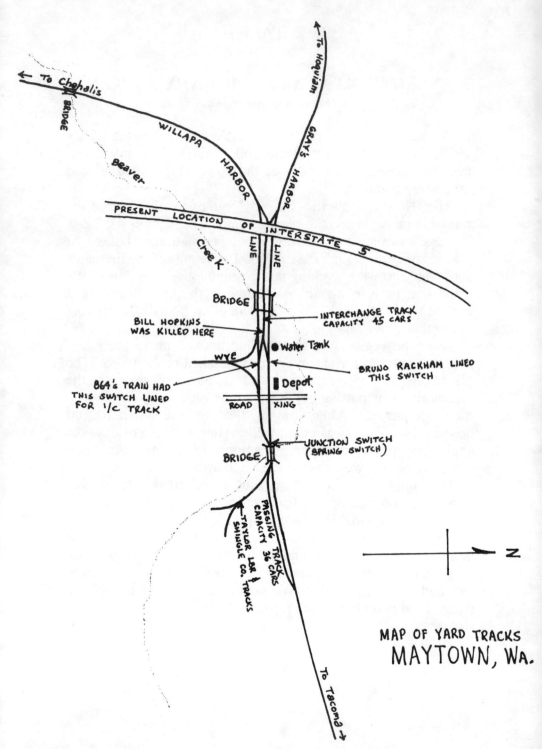

To Hoquiam →

← To Chehalis

BRIDGE

WILLAPA HARBOR

GRAY'S HARBOR

Beaver

PRESENT LOCATION OF INTERSTATE 5

Creek

LINE

LINE

BRIDGE

BILL HOPKINS
WAS KILLED HERE

INTERCHANGE TRACK
CAPACITY 45 CARS

● Water Tank

WYE

BRUNO RACKHAM LINED
THIS SWITCH

864's TRAIN HAD
THIS SWITCH LINED
FOR I/C TRACK

▮ Depot

ROAD XING

JUNCTION SWITCH
(SPRING SWITCH)

BRIDGE

PASSING TRACK
CAPACITY 36 CARS

TAYLOR LBR &
SHINGLE CO. TRACKS

N

MAP OF YARD TRACKS
MAYTOWN, WA.

To Tacoma →

70

RAIL TALES

DEATH AT MAYTOWN
By Leah Rice Carrell - Auburn, Washington

This incident happened around 1936 or 1938 on the Milwaukee Railway at Maytown, Washington. The two trains involved were No. 864 (Longview job) and the Hoquiam Local (No. 862). Both trains were scheduled to leave their terminals at the same time, 6:30 p.m., with the Hoquiam Local arriving Maytown ahead of 864 at 9:30 p.m. Then No. 862 would do their station work, get cars off 864 when it arrived, and depart back to Hoquiam about 12:35 a.m. No. 864 was due into Maytown at 10:45 p.m. to make their setout and pickup, after which they departed for Tacoma.

Maytown was the junction of the Willapa Harbor and Grays Harbor lines, and both lines shared a common interchange track that ran between them (see map).

On the night in question, there was a dense fog in the area, that delayed the Hoquiam Local's arriving Maytown until after 864's arrival. Also a switch light on the interchange track was missing, making it difficult to tell its position in the fog.

Train 864 was in the process of setting out on the interchange track and their brakeman, Bill Hopkins, had lined the switches and was about to give a backup signal to his engineer. Bruno Rackham, brakeman on the Hoquiam Local, No. 862 had lined the switch just west of the boxcar depot for the interchange, not noticing in the thick fog that the other train was already lined into the same track.

When brakeman Hopkins gave the signal to 864, the engineer on the Hoquiam Local took the signal for him and the result was that both trains cornered each other, crushing brakeman Hopkins between cars.

I was a telegrapher at Maytown when this happened. I had just been talking to this young brakeman who was killed a few minutes later, and I knew he was a newly married man with a wife who was expecting their first baby. He was riding the end of a box car when the accident occurred and the impact rolled him, smashed him flat, lantern and all. All I could think of was that I had just been talking to him!

71

65. My parents, Eugene and Carrie Rice visiting me when I lived in the Milwaukee depot at Thorp, Washington about 1926. *Photo, Leah Rice Carrell.*

21. Leah at door of deserted Milwaukee Depot at Auburn, Washington. There were 18 employees during World War II. Leah was the first trick telegrapher.

22. Milwaukee telegrapher, Leah Rice Carrell with son. She celebrated her 100th birthday in 1995.

59. Last Milwaukee Electric engine. *Photo, Bud Emmons*

The conductor came running into the depot all upset.

I said, "Calm yourself, tell me what's wrong so I can call the dispatcher."

The story tumbled from him as he agonized over the details of the shocking accident. After calling the dispatcher on the block phone, I relayed the information to him.

The dispatcher said, "Call the coroner and hold all the trains!" More orders followed as the night wore on.

The conductor on No. 864 was Harry Hendricks. He reluctantly left the dead man on the baggage cart in the freight room, awaiting the arrival of the coroner from Chehalis.

I was due to go off duty at 4:00 a.m. but because the coroner was unable to find Maytown in the fog, I was still on duty at 8:00 a.m. when the depot agent E. W. Hoag came to work. When he arrived, he wanted to know why I was still on duty. I told him about Hopkins and that his body was on the baggage cart in the freight room.

The agent said, "Why didn't you call me?"

I told him, "Why? I'm not afraid of the dead ones, the live ones scare me more. I was only baby-sitting a dead man."

The agent seemed a little amazed that I had the courage to remain at my post with a dead man all night. I told him about the coroner being lost in the fog and that I would stay until he arrived.

The agent took over the train order work and I took a last, unbelieving look at Hopkins in the freight room before sitting down to wait for the coroner. Railroading was never easy.

62. Last run of the Milwaukee Box Car Cab electrics. The photographer chased this train from Easton to Black River, Washington. After this run in 1968 the power was shut off and the overhead line sold for scrap. *Photo, Bud Emmons.*

RAIL TALES

DOG-GONE

By Bill Brandenburg - Sumner, Washington

I was agent for the Northern Pacific Railroad at Sumner, Washington from 1957 to 1967. I remember one afternoon around 5:00 p.m. a young fellow came in with a big dog crate and said he had promised his buddy in the Navy at Whidbey Island he would ship his dog to him. I told him what papers he needed and he brought the dog in the next afternoon. The dog went out by express that evening to join his master in Louisiana.

About three days later, I got a call from the express agent at New Iberia, Louisiana that the arriving dog was a female. The dog shipped was a male! I immediately called the veterinarian who had issued the health certificate, and asked him if the dog was male or female. He said he hadn't really checked the dog but the shipper had said it was a male and that was what he put on the papers.

The express charges were around $65 and we thought the fellow didn't want to pay that price for the wrong dog. Checking further, we found that when they made the transfer at Billings, Montana, the dog got loose. In desperation they ran out in the street and grabbed a dog that looked like the one that got loose, and put it in the crate that was sent on to New Iberia.

With this confession, the express company was now pushed to produce the right dog and they put an ad in the Billings paper offering a reward. In about two weeks a family turned the original dog in to the express company. This dog was sent to his owner and they were back together again.

When I tell this story, everyone asks what happened to the female dog the express company had first sent? I never found out.

RATTLESNAKE VILLAGE:
BECKER, NEW MEXICO
By Glenn E. Young - Flagstaff, Arizona

Becker was located about twenty miles east of Belen terminal on the old Pecos Division of the Santa Fe Railroad. In 1941, it was a twenty-four hour train order station (meaning it never closed) and agency. Becker, famous for its rattlesnake population, kept those who worked there constantly on the lookout for snakes. This was especially true in cold weather, as they would seek out a warm place to stay after sunset.

One December night, I recall it had turned cold early in the evening, and I had to build a good fire in the station "pot-bellied" stove, which made it the warmest place around that particular night. The dispatcher at Clovis rang about 9:30 p.m.

When I answered, his response was, "East, copy four."

It turned out to be a lengthy "wait order" for an eastward freight train on a late westbound passenger train.

About halfway through the order I was copying by hand, for reasons I could not explain, I looked down to my left and saw a snake's head coming up through a hole in the floor where the train order levers worked up and down, as they operated for trains in both directions. It was about a foot away from my left foot. I moved quickly and crawled up on top of the desk and continued to copy and finish the train order. After I repeated the order and got my "complete," I asked dispatcher John Collins for permission to be off the phone because of a snake. By this time, it was about half way into the office and was obviously a large one.

The dispatcher's reply was, "Glenn, forget about that order. Pull in your train order board and get the hell out of there until you get some help to kill that snake!"

I told him I had a plan and would be okay and would get back to him in a few minutes.

The light in the office was extremely poor because of using kerosene lamps. Keeping an eye on the snake in the dim shadows, I slowly slipped off the opposite end of the desk and stepped down onto the floor. The snake saw me and stopped his ascent into the room from underneath the floor. Following my plan, I placed the stove poker into the fire box and in a short time it was red hot. The snake by this time had decided to backtrack, so I had to work fast. I crawled up onto the desk again and leaning over the edge, laid the poker first on the snake's back and then into the opening it was moving back through. I had to admire that reptile as it was being fried to a well-done crisp, but it just kept backing up as painful as it was, until its head and all were pulled by that poker. The smell was overwhelming and the snake shook those floorboards with its rattlers going full blast. I packed paper around the two holes to prevent a re-entry.

This particular incident got a lot of attention as the entire division was waiting to hear whether the telegrapher or the snake won at Becker. Most of them were listening on the phone when I first mentioned the snake. What the heck! What else was there to do at that time of night? Because I was very young on the seniority list, I doubt if too many of them were rooting for the snake in this particular incident.

Later that night Faye Randolf, the third trick telegrapher, who was not afraid of the situation, worked all night with that snake still there. Every time she operated the train order levers to indicate by the position of the board and light on the semaphore pole outside that she had orders for a train, it would sound its rattlers.

Early the next morning, the signal maintainer showed up and got it out. The poker however had done its work, as the snake was just about dead. The rattlers became my possession and while not the largest ever seen, they were large and long for snakes around Becker.

A side note to all this: Faye Randolf had a dog named Bing who delighted in killing rattlesnakes, and he would come to work with Faye every night. It was not uncommon for him to kill several snakes each night. I watched his performance several times. He knew exactly where to grab the snake just behind the head, then shake it back and forth sideways until it was dead.

I didn't stay at Becker very long, but I enjoyed every day I was there, rattlesnakes and all. There is always something special about that first job you could call your very own, especially as a telegrapher.

I later retired from the Santa Fe Railroad as Division Superintendent.

CHIEF LITTLE RAVEN

By Jerry Pratt - Milton, Washington

Years ago, when I worked as Special Agent for the Northern Pacific Railroad in and around the Union Station in Tacoma, Washington, I heard and saw some humorous happenings that helped balance the sad and stark 'other experiences' that daily crossed my path. This is one that broke the monotony and gave us a laugh.

For the convenience of passengers departing from Tacoma for Portland on Train 402, a sleeping car was available on Track 5 at the Union Station. Passengers could board by 9:00 p.m. and relax before departure, which was about midnight.

In this instance, the car was being provided by the Great Northern Railroad and was named for a Blackfoot Indian Chief named "Little Raven."

On the return trip from Portland on Train 401, the generator shaft broke which caused a delay. On arriving at Centralia, a message was sent to the night chief dispatcher, Abe Emmons explaining the delay.

Upon reading the message, Abe calmly announced, "Can you believe this, Chief Little Raven broke his shaft!"

35. NP depot, Jamestown, N.D. Telegraph School was conducted on the second floor of the depot in 1943.

RAIL TALES

MORSE TELEGRAPH SCHOOL
By Ruth Trueblood Eckes - Auburn, Washington

Fresh out of high school in 1943, I was just seventeen and working for a wholesale company across the street from the Union Station in Tacoma, Washington. I saw an ad in the paper that changed my life forever. The Northern Pacific Railway desperate for telegraphers to man their stations because of heavy traffic caused by World War II and a man shortage, was looking for telegraph trainees. Their telegraph school was located in Jamestown, North Dakota and they offered payment of thirty cents an hour, six days a week, eight hours a day to learn. The length of the course lasted about six months, or whenever the trainee qualified as a telegrapher. A job was promised upon completion of qualification of the course.

Well, I jumped on it and went to see about signing up. The chief dispatcher, A. W. Ackley, set things into motion. I was told a physical at the Northern Pacific Benefit Association Hospital in Tacoma, Washington was the first thing to do to see if I was sound in mind and body.

After a few days passed I was accepted for training and one morning with a pass clutched in my hand I boarded the morning connection train out of Tacoma, Washington for East Auburn. There I changed trains to catch No. 4 to Jamestown, North Dakota. I remember having fifteen dollars in my purse and a suitcase of clothes in the baggage car.

My father, Leo Trueblood, was a brakeman for the same railroad and had not said very much to me about my decision. I remembered thinking I saw a slight grin on his face and a twinkle in his eyes when I told him of my plans. My mother wasn't sure a seventeen year old girl could take care of herself but realized it was out of her hands.

When things settled down and the rocking of the train soothed my nerves a little, I began to wonder what I was doing on that train and thought maybe I should have given this adventure more thought. I'd quit my job at the wholesale company and though my boss told me I still had a job if I

83

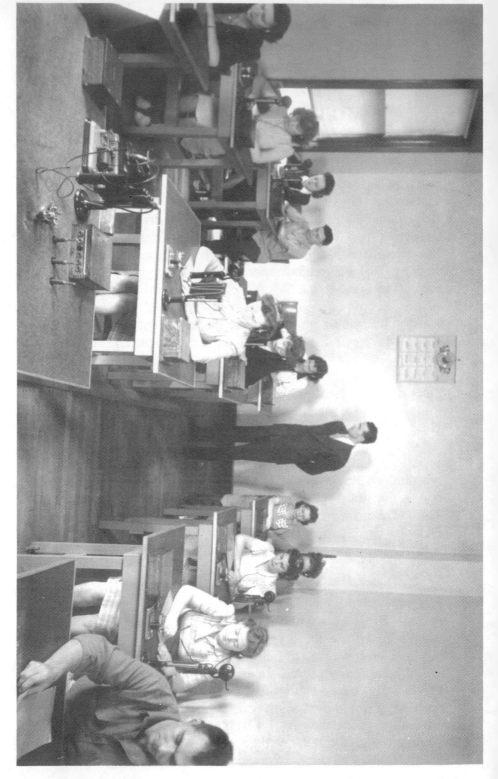

18. Train order class. Instructor Don Hill. *Photo, King Studio - Jamestown, N.D.*

changed my mind and came back, I felt I had burned some bridges and it was now "sink or swim time" for me.

After arriving in Jamestown I found living accommodations in a small private home and my upstairs room rent was $15 a month. The other room upstairs was rented to another telegraph student. Betty Braun was from Dickinson, North Dakota and we shared the bathroom and a little one-burner kerosene stove located in the hallway to cook our meals on.

Our meals were very basic and many times we ate food in the order in which we cooked it. The potatoes first, because they took the longest to cook, then the vegetable, and last the meat. Boiling or frying were our only modes of cookery. Our butter and milk were stored on the windowsill because we lacked an icebox. Milk was delivered by horse and wagon. Gas rationing was in effect making the horse and wagon deliveries "patriotic."

Neither one of us had ever handled money before and the first month we ran out of money and nearly all our food. The only foods on hand were a can of coffee and some potatoes, so we "made do" until payday, about a week away.

The water was hard and nearly undrinkable. Everything we cooked in water had a thick, white scum covering it. It also made washing clothes and dishes difficult. Rainwater was saved in a barrel outside with which to wash our hair.

At school our days were filled with dots and dashes and clattering sounders ringing in our ears. Struggling to make sense of all this was frustrating and we mourned our chances of EVER making sense out of it. But gradually letters and numbers appeared in our strange scratches on paper, and suddenly we began to see words! There were also classes to teach us station accounting, and we learned to copy train orders. We were warned about absolute accuracy when handling train orders as mistakes could cause loss of life. We learned to copy Western Union telegrams and there were strict rules concerning these also.

I had been in school about three months, when one day I found a letter waiting for me in my mailbox telling me to come home. My mother was ill and I was needed.

19. Morse telegraph class. Instructor Guy Rich. *Photo, King Studio - Jamestown, N.D.*

RAIL TALES

Taking my story to Don Hill, manager of the telegraph school was a shock when he refused to give me a train pass to go home, and instead warned me that if I left I wouldn't have the option of returning. They didn't want to spend money on people who didn't stay and complete the course. Without a pass to ride the train I was stranded without money to buy a ticket home.

Panic sent me to ask Mr. Rich (my Morse Code instructor) and my landlord for financial help. Between them I finally got the price of a ticket home, hastily said my goodbyes to class-mates and left town with a heavy heart. I knew I couldn't qualify for a telegraph job on the railroad and my hopes were shattered for a future.

The trip home was interesting though as I forgot I needed money to buy food and my coin purse held only a little change. I miserably wondered how I was going to buy food on the train with no money. Hating to ask for any more help, I decided to tough it out and drink water. I wasn't going to beg.

In my coach there were several Army guards escorting young shell-shocked soldiers home from the war front. They noticed my plight after a while and insisted on sharing their food with me. I gratefully accepted.

Somewhere before dawn in Montana we were jolted awake in our seats when our train hit a broken rail, putting the engine and baggage car on the ground. At dawn the landscape revealed only one lone ranch house a long way off. We waited hours and hours for help, and when it came we were hopelessly late. Our train was annulled and we ran as a passenger extra. We spent time in siding after siding while more important trains were moved across the divisions. We finally arrived in Tacoma over a day late.

When I got home I was happy to find my mother feeling much better and I was again free to make a beginning . . . somewhere. While I was glumly trying to decide what to do, the railroad contacted me. Their solution to my future was to send me to McCarver Street Station in Tacoma to break in under an experienced operator. Before long I received a message to

20. Accounting class. Instructor Mrs. N.M. Mason. *Photo, King Studio - Jamestown, N.D.*

report to a station in the Cascade Mountain foothills and my railroad career was about to begin.

A COW ON THE TRACKS

By Albert Farrow - Auburn, Washington

Many years ago, (about 1938) I was working on the Firemen's extra board out of Auburn on the Northern Pacific Railway. One morning I was called for the "Woolley Local," firing a steam locomotive for Bill Tyner.

From Auburn we followed the double tracks to Black River, where we branched off to single track of the Belt Line Sub-Division. North of Kirkland the single track had scrub trees and brush on both sides of the track — like a jungle laced together with blackberry vines. For several miles there were no grade crossings, but an occasional foot path was cut through the brush. Other than that, it was like a solid wall of green for quite a distance.

Leaving Kirkland, we rounded a curve and immediately applied the brakes and tooted the whistle several times. Up ahead was a black and white cow standing in the middle of the track. As we eased up to the cow with our engine bell ringing and whistle tooting, the cow started up the track away from us. Slowly at first, but as we came closer she took off in a fast gallop. With the whistle tooting and the bell ringing, the engineer opened the steam cylinder cocks hoping to speed the cow on her way.

With head up and nose extended and tail flying straight out, her udder was flopping from side to side, as she tried to keep ahead of this noisy monster that was closing in on her. However, she had no intention to crash through the wall of brush on either side of the track.

Finally after about a mile of this chase, the cow came to a foot path and quickly made an exit through the brush and disappeared. No doubt some farmer had problems getting his herd together that evening.

50. Wayne Baldwin, wire chief for the Morse Telegraph Club, Evergreen Chapter in Tacoma, Washington. Morse demonstration, Model Railroad show in Seattle, Washington, 1994. *Photo, Ed Eckes.*

RAIL TALES

I'M LEAVING RIGHT NOW!
By Wayne Baldwin - Seattle, Washington

The depot at Kanaskat, Washington on the Northern Pacific Railway was probably built about 1900, and was a good sized, two story frame structure, with the usual telegraph office, baggage room and storage area on the first floor. The upper floor was living quarters for the agent and operators.

In the early 1940s, the Agent, Stan Edwall, had his own home nearby so the upper floor was used by the second and third trick operators. It also housed extra board folks who worked in the area, even if they were not assigned at "GV"— Kanaskat. I remember that Bill Wallace and I worked some tricks at Kanaskat and nearby offices such as "AY"— Auburn Yard, "AU" — Auburn Depot, "SN"— Sumner, "KN"— Kent, and "PY"— Puyallup. This was for economic reasons because the extra board telegrapher and relief agents had absolutely no expense allowance in those days and during those years many of us called Kanaskat home.

Well, this wonderful old depot was accidentally burned to the ground in either the late fall or winter of 1943. The exact date is unavailable.

On this cold winter night a young operator by the name of Gordon Trehanus, about eighteen years old, was working third trick (12:01 a.m. to 8:00 a.m.) at Kanaskat. He had built up a good fire in the coal stove of the depot and then went to sleep some time around 1:00 in the morning.

The stove overheated from the heavy coal fire while Gordon was asleep and caught the office on fire. Gordon woke up at this point and called the train dispatcher on the dispatcher's phone. I happened to be working close by at Auburn Yard, and was sending a consist on the Morse wire to Yakima Yard, but was plugged into the train dispatcher's phone line and had the earphones on my head, when I heard the following:

"DISPATCHER, KANASKAT! DISPATCHER, KANASKAT! THE STATION IS ON FIRE AND I AM LEAVING RIGHT NOW!"

57. Kanaskat NP Depot built in 1900 and burned down in 1943. People unknown. *Courtesy, Museum of History & Industry, Seattle, WA.*

38. NP Extra 6005 west of Kanaskat, Washington July 15, 1945.
Depot in background was built after the original depot burned. It was
abandoned in 1959 after the line changed. *Photo, Ed Eckes.*

37. Last Kanaskat depot built after main line was relocated. Agent Ernie Harrison (in pictures) eventually bought the depot from the Burlington Northern Railroad. *Photo, Ed Eckes.*

Apparently Gordon woke up in time to save his life. I remember a short conversation he had with the trick dispatcher, and then the trick dispatcher's phone started "crackling" and there was no more communication. I wish I could remember the name of that dispatcher.

Gordon was the son of a section foreman who worked on the Northern Pacific. I believe Gordon came out of the Spokane Telegraph School during World War II, along with many others at this time when the railroads were hiring newly trained telegraphers.

Sam Watterson, a retired Northern Pacific and Burlington Northern Railway engineer, remembers being on an eastbound freight train, probably 602, that was stopped at Kanaskat the morning of the fire. The dispatcher, of course, put out a stop order on all train traffic moving in both directions on this important main line between Auburn and Yakima. Sam recalled being stopped for several hours along with other trains until it was safe to move traffic again.

Engine 2603 on passenger train No. 408 leaving King St. Station, Seattle in 1946
Photo: Albert Farrow

34. NP temporary station at Kanaskat, Washington, March 18, 1945. Agent/telegrapher Stan Edwall in doorway with Don. *Photo, J.M. Fredrickson.*

RAIL TALES

DON, MY RAILROAD DOG
By Ruth Trueblood Eckes - Auburn, Washington

Fresh out of the Jamestown, North Dakota Telegraph School in 1944, my first 'solo' job on the Northern Pacific Railroad was at Kanaskat, Washington located in the Cascade Mountain foothills. The depot had burned down and the railroad moved in an outfit car to replace it. Half of it was the telegraph office and the other half the waiting room. The little town consisted of a few houses, a store, tavern and the depot.

My living quarters were not much better. The only housing available was a one room cabin in the woods, located about a mile from the depot. The inside of the cabin was 'make do' with a couple of cupboards on the wall for supplies, a few pots and pans, a small sink, bed, table, two chairs and an old wood and coal range for heat and cooking.

The back door led into a wood shed containing fuel for the stove. My bathtub was a big washtub hanging on a nail. Any hot water for doing dishes or taking a bath was heated in pots and pans on the stove. The outhouse was behind the cabin under a tree. Trips after dark required a flashlight in order to find it. The house did have electric lights — one light globe in the ceiling.

My work shift was third trick (12:01 a.m. to 8:00 a.m.) and my walk to work at the depot was at midnight along a trail bordering the tracks. Luckily I was not afraid of the dark.

I was only seventeen and didn't know a soul in town. I worked seven days a week and couldn't get out of town except by train. Passenger train No. 3 from the east had to be late enough coming through Kanaskat for me to catch it home to Tacoma, Washington. After working all night, I'd go without sleep all day and return on the evening passenger train (No. 6) to go to work again.

Being alone in the depot each night was a little terrifying and responsibility hung heavy over me as I was learning to depend on myself and there was nobody to ask questions of. It was either do the work correctly or get fired. The deputy sheriff from Enumclaw kept an eye on me though and would either call

97

by phone or stop by to see if I was all right almost every night. Sometimes he even arrived with a hot hamburger and a milkshake!

There were men everywhere — a work gang with men from Mexico who didn't speak English, an extra gang, loggers, train crews, a signal maintainer and lineman who were on call every time there was trouble with signals or telegraph wires. It was winter time and some of the men who boarded the trains going east had snowshoes strapped to their backs and were dressed in warm outdoor clothes.

I had been warned about railroaders and was told not to be gullible. Stan Edwall, Agent at Kanaskat, knew from the start that he had a young, green, female operator on his hands who didn't know much about railroading or life. He tried hard to tell me what my duties were. He outlined my job description in detail that included checking the yard, sweeping the depot floor, dumping the ashes and many other tasks, but first of all came the train order and telegraph work. At first I wasn't sure how much I should believe, but Stan was patient and finally convinced me. His Swedish accent still rings in my ears when he snapped, "Rutie, that's a box car, not a refrigerator car!"

My yard check was sometimes incomplete as I couldn't find all the cars in the dark of third trick and Stan in exasperation finally drew a map of the yard naming the tracks for me. I became a weigh master and weighed coal cars when the local train came off the branch line after midnight. The engineer would pull the cars in the train over the scale one at a time, and each would have to be weighed and a little card made out showing the car number and tonnage.

My world was full of learning new things. I learned to tie slip knots in the strings that held the train orders which were threaded onto "Y" shaped hoops. One hoop readied for the head of the train and one for the rear. My duties also included a "roll-by" check of each train to spot hot boxes (journal boxes that caught fire) or anything dragging under the train.

The sign for a hot box differed as to where it was located in the train. If it was near the head end of the train, you held your nose and patted your head. In the middle of the train, you held your nose and patted your stomach. That left the rear of the train and as you probably guessed, called for holding your nose and patting your fanny. It was embarrassing at first but later just part of the job. If something was dragging, you dragged your hand or lantern (if at night) along on the ground and the crew knew instantly what those signs meant and took proper action to remedy the situation.

New experiences included an incident which scared me enough to think I needed protection. A few nights before this incident, the branch line crew was waiting for me at a road crossing when I reached the tracks on my way to work at midnight.

Without explaining, they just said, "Ruth, get on the engine and we'll give you a ride up to the depot."

I persisted in knowing why, and they finally said it was payday and it would be safer for me to ride the engine than walk to work. The work gang was drunk, rowdy, and looking for trouble.

I didn't worry about this information at the time until a few nights later when I was checking the yard before dawn, and the gang from Mexico surrounded me as I wrote down a boxcar number. Glancing over my shoulder I saw them silently and ominously watching me and I froze. I was afraid to show fear, so I continued to write the boxcar number on my yard check and appeared busy and unconcerned. As they moved slowly in on me, shivers went up my spine and I wondered what to do. About the time I decided to scream for help, I heard the gang foreman come around one of the outfit cars and in rapid but brief Spanish ordered them away.

My parents hearing of this incident, decided I needed a dog for protection and arrived soon with a big German Police dog named Don. Don, came from the dog pound and they didn't know much about him except he looked vicious and protective. They left him with me and he wouldn't even answer to his name. He didn't particularly like me and I returned the favor. I wondered how we were going to get along as we couldn't meet on common ground.

The Cabin. *Photo, Ruth Eckes*.

Ted Drake, second trick telegrapher.

Don. *Photo, Ruth Eckes*.

RAIL TALES

Regardless of how he felt about me though, he walked me to work each night and spent eight hours keeping me company in the depot. I was glad to have him, except one night he scared a passenger by chewing on the man's white shoes and daring him to do something about it. The frightened man offered no opposition and was glad to escape when the train came while I held Don by the collar long enough for him to run out the door. After that incident I chained Don to the safe each night!

Little by little this big, burley dog's personality revealed many things to me. He was strong-minded and an independent thinker, but had a sense of humor that cropped up at odd times and kept me on my toes anticipating his reactions to things happening in our daily lives. He also gradually took on the responsibility of protecting me and HE decided when that was necessary.

His reputation grew rapidly as more incidents occurred. One morning after work I stopped at the local store for groceries. The door didn't close all the way and he pushed into the store behind me to keep an eye on what I was doing. I turned and pointed for him to wait outside just as a man was coming through the door. Don leaped for the man's throat, thinking I had given him the sign to attack. The man threw his arm up to protect himself and Don clamped his teeth around it. I called Don off and apologized. We headed for home without the groceries. Now that I knew Don's training may have been by the army, I knew I needed to be more careful in the future.

One night at work, I had just copied an order for a freight train east out of Auburn that was pulling up to the water tank to take water on the steam engine. The head brakeman burst through the door to pickup the engineer's orders and reached across the typewriter, grabbing me by the shoulders. I started to draw back, feeling instant alarm, and saw his face not more than four inches from mine, rapidly turn white as the color ebbed away.

I heard him gasp, "Ruth, call off your dog!"

Don sensing danger, swiftly and firmly gripped his teeth around the man's arm. His low, savage growl showed he meant business. He swiftly defended me without being told. When

Don released him, the brakeman fled hastily out the door with his orders clutched in his hand.

As time went by, Don and I became good friends and I relied on him as my best friend. Nobody ever got out of line with me. His reputation was solid and everybody respected him.

As summer came on, sleeping days in that little cabin was intolerable and we hiked up to the Green River Headwork's Dam. We slept on the grass by the river in the shade of one of the buildings. Nobody ever warned us away or bothered us. We would share a tuna fish or peanut-butter sandwich before walking back down the dusty road along the river in the late afternoon. Sometimes we stopped to soak our feet in the cold water and he loved to run off with my stockings that were never seen again.

In life, all things change and rarely do they continue to be the same for very long. Don's life ended in the Stampede Tunnel shortly after I was suddenly sent to work at Yakima. I couldn't take him with me, so the night operator at Stampede borrowed him for company. For some unexplained reason, Don ran into the mouth of the tunnel just as the section foreman and crew were coming out of the tunnel on their track car. They hit him and killed him. When somebody called me on the phone telling me the news, I knew I had lost my best friend and I grieved over him for a long time.

SEATTLE WAS MY FUTURE

By Edward Khatain - Edmonds, Washington

After finishing relief work at the Great Northern Railway's Whitefish, Montana dispatcher's office, I headed west in 1943. It was late summer and I boarded No. 27 (the fast mail) one morning and rode to the west coast to seek my fortune.

At Spokane, Washington a young operator boarded the train who introduced himself to me as Bill Webb (later to become Car Distributor in Seattle) and stated that he too was going to Seattle. We chatted away into the night about the current state of affairs, railroading in general and most importantly, about girls. All of this nonsense talk was embellished by the contents of a familiar bottle which magnified the conversation by leading to half-truths and outright lies. We made a pact that we would stick together and take off for Alaska to determine if there was any substance to the tales of the far north.

After our arrival in Seattle, while threading our way through a very busy and crowded waiting room, I said to Bill, "Why don't you sit down for a few minutes while I run upstairs to see what the extra work, if any, is like; merely to satisfy my curiosity, then I'll be right back."

I walked into the dispatcher's office thinking this venture probably was a waste of time on everybody's part when I confronted Heinie Wellein for the first time. Heinie was the chief dispatcher and he sized me up.

Then with a resounding slam of his fist onto his old hardwood desk he stated, "Yes, a shortage of dispatchers certainly does exist and I want you to immediately go into the coast-line booth and commence breaking in with Roy Van Dyke."

Roy was working the Seattle to Vancouver, B.C. district that day. I agreed to do this but was so non-pulsed by the entire chain of events that I completely forgot poor Bill Webb, still waiting downstairs.

It was going to be about twenty years before I would see Bill again and the first thing he asked me was, "What happened to you Ed? After about two hours I got tired of waiting for you to

2. Ed Khatain, telegraph demonstration at Model Railroad Show in Seattle Science Center, 1993. *Photo, Ed Eckes*

show and left, not for Alaska but back to the Spokane Division as an operator."

I had to tell him then that I hadn't made it to Alaska either, but continued working as a dispatcher in the Seattle office until 1967, when I was promoted to the position of Chief Dispatcher. There had been three others who had filled this position between Heinie's retirement and my appointment, which I held for fourteen years, until my retirement in 1981.

I certainly respected Heinie Wellein and felt he belonged to a different day and age. He was no phony!

A SQUEAL FOR DEAR LIFE
By Bill Brandenburg - Sumner, Washington

When I was agent at Bothell, Washington in 1954, working for the Northern Pacific Railroad, a party brought in a pig to ship via express and another party brought in two mink to ship. A while later, the truck driver picked up the pig and the two mink and headed for Seattle, Washington.

About three miles out of Bothell, he heard a terrible commotion in the back of his truck. The pig was squealing for dear life. The alarmed and puzzled truck driver pulled into a service station to see what was wrong. He discovered the crates were too close together and the pig's tail waved over the two mink's crate and one of the mink grabbed it and wouldn't let go. The poor pig went right on squealing and the truck driver didn't know what to do to make the mink let go.

A helpful and amused onlooker at the service station offered advise. He said to throw a pail of water in the mink's face and it would probably let go. Desperate for a solution, they got a pail of water and threw it in the mink's face. It did let go and the pig stopped squealing. The pig was none the worse for his experience except for two tooth holes in his tail and hurt feelings. The two mink got a free bath and all three arrived in Seattle safely.

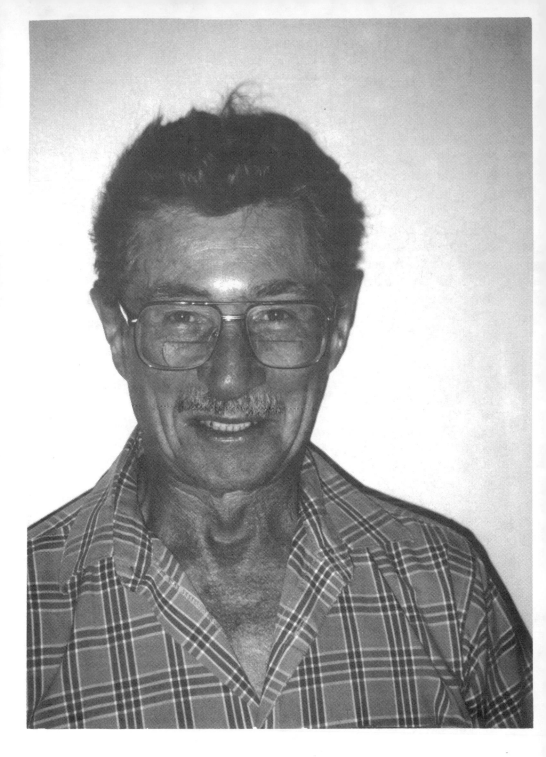

40. Canadian Pacific Railroad Engineer, John O. Stanley. *Photo, John O. Stanley.*

A COLD CLIMB

By John O. Stanley - Whittier, California

I remember an occasion from early in my years as a fireman for the Canadian Pacific Railroad when I was scheduled on a run west to Field, British Columbia. I always appreciated the runs to the west as all the engines were stoker or oil burners except the Way Freight run.

We found our engine would be number 5432, a fairly new engine, only three and a half years old. The month was January and we were in the middle of a cold spell, and I was more than pleased to draw engine 5432 as it was a closed cab engine. The engineer I drew for the trip had a reputation for working the hell out of the engines and sometimes the firemen too.

Everything seemed to be going smoothly but I could see that I would have to crowd the stoker a bit and run the water pump at a good clip also to just keep up with the engineer's hard running. We stopped for water at Canmore and had a meet with a train there before heading out onto the main track for our destination at Field, British Columbia.

We had started this trip about 4:00 p.m. and it was now two hours later on a very dark, cold winter day. I was feeling proud of myself for keeping up with the heavy hand of the engineer when a few miles outside of Banff the steam gauge started to drop and I immediately jumped down and opened the firebox door. I discovered the stoker was not churning any coal and the engineer immediately figured the coal had frozen in the tender. He instructed me to take the scoop shovel and climb out his door, get up on the tender and break loose the frozen coal.

We were traveling about thirty miles per hour and the instructions astonished me. If we had been stopped it would have been no problem but at thirty miles per hour I felt I had a BIG problem. I still don't believe I did it, but yes I did climb out of the cab and with the handle of the scoop shovel hanging on my arm, reached for rungs on the tender and slowly started climbing. It was about then that reality set in and I knew if I

107

44. Engine 5923, Westbound on No. 3. Field, B.C., May 22, 1946.
Oil burner engine. *Photo, R.V. Nixon*

45. Engine 2378 at Edmonton, Alberta on No. 526, Southbound to Calgary. Picture taken May 20, 1946. Stoker fired engine. *Photo, R.V. Nixon*

43. Double header on passenger train No. 2, Eastbound and climbing Field Hill, June 1929. *Photo, R.V. Nixon*

42. Engine 2366 at Edmonton, Alberta, May 20, 1946. Stoker fired.
Photo, R.V. Nixon

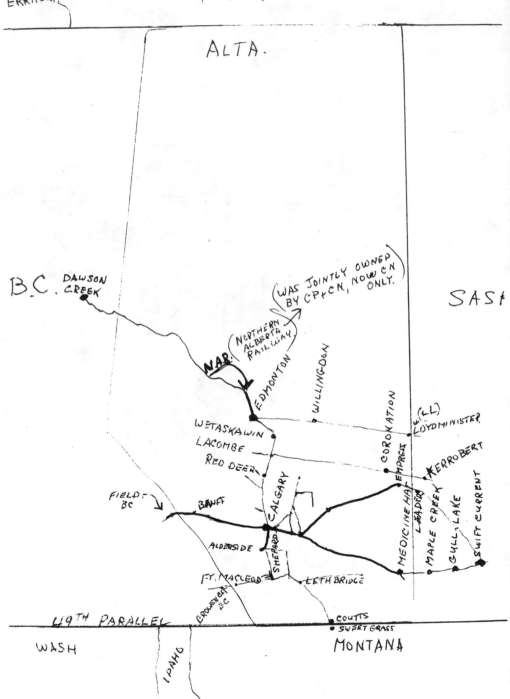

were to fall off I'd die and no one would care. WHAT A THOUGHT!

I finally made it to the top of the tender and reached over with the scoop and began to break up the frozen coal. Another thought occurred to me about having to crawl into the coal bunker; if I slipped while the worm was turning, I hated to think what my fate might be. Unhappy thoughts churned in my head and I wondered what the outcome would be before I again reached the safety of the cab.

A little while later I had coal sliding down into the lower part of the tender and knew the worm was carrying it into the firebox as cinders started hitting my face. I slowly moved over to the rungs on the side of the tender and climbed down the side and into the cab.

With the engine traveling at thirty miles per hour and the breeze biting into me I was nearly frozen. Thinking about this experience later made me feel that the safety of railroad men was not a big factor in those days. Of course, the engineer was glad to see me back safely in the cab and thanked me for my efforts. I was thinking how thankful I was to make it back alive and to be inside that warm, safe cab.

56. Pacific Coast Railroad No. 16 starting up the branch line at Maple Valley, Washington Sept. 14, 1951. Virgil Ungherini, fireman. Bill Anthony on the steps. *Photo, Al Farrow.*

SMOKE SIGNALS

By Bill Harshfield - Maple Valley, Washington

The Maple Valley depot in the '50s was the dispatcher's office for all Pacific Coast trains on the Pacific Coast Railroad tracks between Maple Valley and Seattle, Washington. The train dispatchers were also operators for all Milwaukee Railroad trains heading east for Saint Paul, Minnesota. Of course that meant the depot was manned twenty-four hours a day.

This building was a large, two story, wood frame building with a freight shed on the east end and a passenger waiting room on the west end, with living quarters on the upper floor above the dispatcher's office and the waiting room

Jack Shuman was the on-coming first trick dispatcher and the first thing he did upon entering the office was to hang up his coat and check the fire in the old pot-bellied stove which stood in the middle of the office.

Well, the third trick dispatcher apparently had been very busy with train orders and track lineups at that time of morning, and neglected putting some of that good Utah coal in the stove. It was a cold, crisp morning in Maple Valley and time for the shift change in the depot, when this occurred.

Dave Rose was second trick dispatcher, he and his wife lived upstairs. Dave and his very pious wife were in their late fifties. Dave got off at twelve midnight and usually didn't get to bed until 1:00 or 2:00 a.m., so naturally he didn't get up very early in the morning. The living quarters were modern in all respects and the bedroom where the Rose's slept had a brick chimney that came from the dispatcher's office, up through the bedroom and out the roof. In the brick chimney was a stove pipe hole that had one of those old fashioned thimble tin plates with the springs in the back to hold them in place. It was covering the hole because they no longer needed a stove upstairs for heat. Directly under that stove hole was where Mrs. Rose chose to

115

Maple Valley Depot. *Warren Wing Collection.*

put the bed. On this particular morning it had a lavish bed spread covering it.

John noticed the fire was getting very low and almost out. He picked up the coal bucket which was sitting next to the stove and proceeded to dump about half a bucket of fuel in on top of the few remaining red coals in the stove, causing them to be almost smothered.

John took his seat and the transfer was made. The third trick dispatcher left for home. Shortly after this transaction a tremendous pouf from the stove was heard and the stove door flew open. Smoke poured into the office and the fire started to burn briskly again.

It was at this time, feet hit the floor upstairs and pounded down the stairs to the office. If you could have seen Dave's face it was probably scarlet under the soot, he was so mad! When the smothered fire got air and blew up, it blew the thimble out of the chimney and soot all over the bed.

If ever a man was berated it was John, as Dave really gave it to him. Dave was not normally a swearing man but he sure knew all the words that morning. (He probably learned them all from the "gandies.")

Eventually Dave calmed down and peace was restored in the Maple Valley depot. Needless to say the B&B crew (Bridge and Building) were on the job the next day with a couple of bricks and a bucket of cement, permanently sealing up that hole.

HOOP PROBLEMS

By Leah Rice Carrell - Auburn, Washington

I had just started work as a telegrapher in 1918 for the Milwaukee Railroad in Othello, Washington. I was working extra, relieving at different stations along the line. The chief wanted me to relieve the girls on the night shift. Hurley, my husband, who was stationed at Othello, where we lived, had gone upstairs to bed in the depot.

Before going he had said, "You will be able to handle the job okay."

We always had a bunch of hoops hanging on the wall and the extra hoops were out in the freight shed. There was a freight due out of Othello soon.

Hurley had advised, "When you see the headlight, the dispatcher will send orders for the train."

When the chief dispatcher called, he said, "Don't stop this freight train. I want you to hoop up an order to them to meet the passenger train at Jerico."

I got the orders ready and reached up to get a hoop — and there were no hoops!

I said, "Oh my God! Where are the hoops?"

I yelled to Hurley, "Where are the hoops, where are the hoops, where are the hoops!"

Hurley awakened and called down, "The hoops are in the freight house overhead."

I went up that ladder six steps at a time, unlocked the door, and grabbed the bundle of hoops. Throwing them down, I grabbed one and ran out the door and hooped up the order just as the train went by. I was shaking all over.

The next morning Hurley asked, "What the hell was the matter with you last night?"

I replied, "You left me without any hoops."

He said, "I didn't know there weren't any hoops."

I told Hurley how it scared me to death, because the chief didn't want me to stop that train and it looked like I was going to anyway, if I didn't find some hoops . . . in a hurry.

118

RAIL TALES

RAILROAD NIGHT CALLS
By Jack R. Sage - Steilacoom, Washington

When I went to work for the Northern Pacific Railway for the signal department on June 10, 1946, I began the equivalent of a second competing marriage. For the next thirty-five years I was subject to being called to duty twenty-four hours a day. The only time I had that I was free was when I was on vacation out of town.

Many times I would just be sitting down to a special dinner with my family, celebrating birthdays, holidays, etc., when the phone would ring. It would be the dispatcher calling me out to trouble-shoot some signal problem on the railroad. Most of the calls seemed to come after I had gone to bed. Occasionally these calls would interrupt some of those intimate relationships. I wouldn't be too cheerful on those occasions.

Sometimes these calls would be caused by tragedies along the railroad right-of-way. On one occasion I had just started to eat my dinner. The phone rang. There had been a train-car accident on a crossing near Toppenish. Five young men in an automobile had tried to beat a diesel-freight to the crossing and lost. The boys had been on their way to a school dance. The automobile was thrown into one of our automatic block signals, causing heavy damage to the signal equipment. Four of the youths were killed instantly, and the fifth died later in a hospital.

While we were making repairs, some of the surviving relatives came by to pick up the youth's dress shoes to use at the funerals. It was very sad for all of us. When I returned home I had lost my appetite for the big dinner.

Whenever there was an accident on a signalized highway crossing, I would be called out to test the signals in front of disinterested witnesses. One time, very late at night, I was called to the Steilacoom Blvd. crossing near the Mountain View Cemetery. I stopped a passing car and asked the occupants if they would be willing to witness me testing the signals. The couple said okay but they were hoping they wouldn't have to appear later in court. I assured them that would unlikely be necessary. They gave me their names and addresses. They were married, but not to each other.

The stormier the weather the more likely that I would be called out. On most of my trouble calls I had to use a track car to reach the trouble spot. Running the track car at night was a hazard in itself, not only from trains (I lost two track cars to trains in my thirty-five years) but also danger from trespassers.

Vandals would often place objects on the rails which would derail the track car. I was injured a few times from these actions.

Animals were another hazard, especially deer on the tracks which would be attracted by the car's headlights. Sometimes on night calls, if the moon happened to be out, I would run the track car without my headlights. This could be a little scary especially if I was traveling about fifty miles per hour in the dark.

One time I was working in Eastern Washington and I accidentally hit a badger with the track car. I got off the car to see if it was okay, and it ran back to the car snapping and snarling at my legs.

One night I was called to Solo Point and found one of my slide-detector fences was missing. I heard noises on the beach and found a couple of young soldiers at a party with their girl friends. They were using the wood from the fence for a bonfire. I called the military police to come to the area to take care of the situation. They did and supposedly took the names of the soldiers. However, the names were missing the next day for our railroad police.

Mud slides were also a hazard and I had fifteen miles of slide-detector fences to maintain on my territory. Quite often after a mud slide had covered the tracks the fences had to be rebuilt. Trees were often brought down in the slides and damage was done to the pole line as well. I kept in fairly good shape with the exercise of digging fence post holes and climbing the poles to repair signal wires.

Train derailments kept me busy at times. Many of these accidents seemed to happen at night when not many employees were able to check the passing trains for "hot-boxes" and other possible hazards. At the derailments I usually had to wait until the tracks were repaired before I could do my work. Consequently, I spent a lot of time waiting to get started on my own repair work.

Since I spent so much time waiting, and usually there were no places nearby to eat, I had emergency snacks with me. I kept soup mixes, tea, crackers, canned beans and other items for those long waiting periods.

Most of my calls in over the twenty years I worked out of Steilacoom took place after midnight when the second trick dispatchers came on duty. I used to accuse the dispatchers of doing these things on purpose, since they also had to be awake, they thought I should be too. Usually after I took care of the trouble along the line, I didn't get much sleep before having to go back on the job at the regular time. It wasn't too easy to get used to but I did this for over thirty-five years. I still seemed to have time to do volunteer work for my church and the community at large. I was active on the Steilacoom town council for four of my twelve years as a council member.

Now that I'm retired, I enjoy the lack of frozen or wet feet, rain-soaked body, wind and sand-burned face, cinders in my eyes, and fatigue after long hours of working.

12. Ed Eckes, standing in front of the south end of the Auburn Diesel House, 1980, Burlington Northern Railroad. *Photo, Ed Eckes.*

RAIL TALES

THE GOOD AND THE BAD
By Eddie Eckes - Auburn, Washington

This title refers to road jobs or repairs to locomotives that have broken down away from the repair shops. My job as machinist on the Northern Pacific Railway took me to some remote locations and miserable situations during my many years of helping to keep them in running shape.

The first one that comes to mind was not long before I had finished my apprenticeship as a machinist in 1951. I was set up to machinist a few months before this and was not very experienced.

A W3 class 'Mike' locomotive had broken a spring hanger and was sitting on a siding at the small town of Woodinville, Washington. My helper, Bill Krone, and I reported for work at the roundhouse in Auburn, Washington at 11:00 p.m. on the graveyard shift. The roundhouse foreman told us to get our tools together for the trip to Woodinville. We were slated for a trouble-shooting job.

We went to the storehouse and picked up a new spring hanger and loaded every tool we thought we might need into my old 1940 Dodge coupe. (The Northern Pacific Railroad at that time didn't seem to have a truck available for us to use, so we had to use our own cars.)

We headed up north to the trouble site at Woodinville, Washington and arrived about an hour and a half later. This was winter time and naturally it was raining a cold hard rain. We soon discovered the broken spring hanger was the front hanger of the left number one driver.

The front of the spring was jammed up into the boiler jacket. The problem would be to get enough slack in the rigging to put in the new hanger. This was easier said than done. The usual method in the shops would be to run the number one drivers and wheels up on wedges. (This is a tapered steel wedge that is about three to four inches thick at the large end and about three inches wide and about a yard long in length -- weighing about fifty pounds.) After putting some steel blocking between the top of the driving boxes and the frame and blocking the spring

123

14. Machine shop, Auburn Diesel House. *Photo, Ed Eckes.*

equalizers, the engine is run down off the wedges. A short section of rail is taken out and the wheel is dropped into the opening. This should give slack in the spring rigging.

But out there on a repair job there isn't any short section of rail to take out, so it is much harder to get the needed slack. These were almost always hard, difficult jobs that could be dangerous and miserable if the weather was bad.

The first problem showed up when we tried to run the engine up on the wedges. The engineer would slowly move the engine onto the wedges. Part way up, the wedges would fly out from under the wheels. This was a time to watch where you were standing, because if a wedge hit you it could break a leg. The small rail on the siding was rounded and wet from the rain, which made it slippery. We put sand on the rail and wedge and it helped somewhat.

We had to go through this operation many times before we had enough slack to replace the hanger. Each time when the engine was up on the wedges, I had to climb over the driver wheels and crawl between the boiler and the frame, and down onto the brake rigging to add more blocking to keep the frame up farther off the driving boxes. My only consolation was that it was warmer and dryer in there.

Once the slack was obtained, the next problem showed up. The hanger wouldn't fit through the slot in the spring, so the only thing to do was get out the file and file it down so that it would fit in place. While all this was going on, someone would come over from the depot every couple of hours, to ask when the engine would be ready.

After finally getting the hanger to fit, putting in the hanger pin, spring gib and cotter keys, we had to go all through the process of running the engine up on wedges, removing all the blocking, and finally it was done.

The operator at the depot was notified that the engine was ready to run. We picked up our tools and headed back to Auburn. A job that might have taken a couple of hours in the roundhouse had stretched out to about twelve hours and it was about 1:00 p.m. when we got back. I would consider this a bad job.

13. Blacksmith's steam hammer and tools. Auburn Roundhouse –
1980 – Burlington Northern Railroad. *Photo, Ed Eckes.*

RAIL TALES

The next road job that I recall happened not long after the one at Woodinville. I was still on graveyard shift when my helper, Harry Rhine, and I were called to go to Renton, Washington where another Mike W3 had broken down. It had a broken right trailer truck wheel. This time the road foreman took us down to Renton where the engine was parked. It was headed north near the Boeing Aircraft plant. Luckily for us, the afternoon shift machinist had the broken wheel tied up with a chain, clear of the track, so all we had to do was have the engineer back the engine toward Black River. The next move was to put it on the mainline track toward Auburn and to move it to the shop for repairs. Having found out from the last job, I wasn't too surprised to find that things don't always go as well as you think they should.

As soon as we started backing the engine up, we found out why things wouldn't happen as planned. Having no flanged wheel on the right side trailer truck, the left wheel would derail after just a few feet of moving the engine. This would entail removing the rerailing frog from the side of the tender, putting it under the derailed wheel and running the engine forward each time the wheel was derailed. We also tried oiling the rail ahead of the wheel. This helped some, but the wheel continued derailing every so often. With at least two or three miles to Black River, this was getting to be a long hard job. After many, many rerailing episodes over the next several hours, we finally reached Black River Junction.

I think my helper and I carried that damn rerailing frog (which weighed at least seventy- five to one hundred pounds) most of the way from the Boeing plant in Renton to Black River that night. Stumbling in the ballast alongside that engine in the dark was not much fun.

At Black River the engine was backed onto the north leg of the wye, which headed it toward Auburn on the main line. It was to our advantage, because with the engine headed forward, the wheel tended to stay on the rail a lot better. After watching it for a while to be sure, we climbed into the cab and took off for Auburn at about ten miles per hour. Once in the yard at Auburn the engine had to be backed to the roundhouse and we

15 Diesel traction motors. *Photo, Ed Eckes.*

ran into the same situation again. The wheel wouldn't stay on the rail and out came the oil can and the rerailing frog again. After about ten hours from the time we first started moving the engine, it rolled into the roundhouse.

One of the next road repair jobs came in the early 1960s. A freight diesel locomotive on No. 675 (a train that ran from Auburn to Sumas, near the Canadian border), had derailed south of Deming, Washington. The wrecking crew was putting the units back on the rails and my job was to put in a new drawbar between the A and B units. The wrecking crew had been forced to cut the drawbar in order to rerail the units.

Harold Krie (my helper) and I were called to work early in the morning, as we were working the day shift at that time. We borrowed the rip track truck that had a small lift crane in back and loaded a new drawbar and all the tools we thought we could use. Then we headed for Deming about one hundred miles north of Auburn.

Arriving in Deming about 10:00 a.m., we found the wrecking crew had one unit of the locomotive on a siding in town, so we pulled the truck over by the unit and looked over the job. The drawbar had been cut off with an acetylene torch and the remainder of the drawbar was still in place in the unit. The drawbar pin (a steel pin about six inches in diameter and eighteen inches long) had to be pulled up, its keeper bar removed and then the drawbar pin dropped to the ground. Then the drawbar centering device had to be swung out of the way, a cable attached to the drawbar and the drawbar pulled out of the pocket to the ground. After the old drawbar was out of the way, the truck was backed up next to the end of the unit and the drawbar was picked up by the crane and gently pushed into place. The pin was replaced and secured by the gib and cotter key and the centering device put back in place.

The drawbar measures about six inches wide by five inches thick and about eight feet long. The ends where the pins fit through, are about a foot wide and have bearings installed to permit it to swivel when going around curves. It probably weighs at least a half ton and is of solid steel.

16. Diesel Wheels. *Photo, Ed Eckes.*

RAIL TALES

The foregoing part of the job didn't take very long so we had lunch and waited for the wrecking crew to bring the other unit from the site of the derailment.

This was wintertime and there were snow patches on the ground. Though the sun was out, there was a real chill in the air and we built a small fire to keep warm, while waiting for the other unit.

Finally, the other unit came around the curve from the south. It was coupled to nine box cars and was pushed by a GP unit. It entered the siding and the crew stopped it near the other unit. The other half drawbar had to be removed like the first half before proceeding with the rest of the job. I didn't like going between the units with the power unit so far away, but decided to try it anyway. I had to go between the two units and between the rails. With a small bar, I pried the end of the drawbar up to align it with the drawbar pocket, while the units were pushed together. This was a time to be careful as I was positioned in a spot where I could have been caught between the units and crushed.

The engineer was given the come ahead signal, I aligned the drawbar and it slid into position perfectly. The unit was uncoupled from the rest of the train, the drawbar pin put into place, securing the centering device in place, and the job was done. This was one job that everything went very well and there were no problems.

We loaded up our tools and headed for home, stopping in Sedro Woolley for dinner. We arrived back in Auburn about 9:00 p.m. that night. This was about a fourteen hour job.

Another road job that happened sometime in the 1970s involved a GP-9 engine just west of Thorp, Washington. It had died on the main line while headed west and the passenger train was due in a little over two hours.

Joe Wagner, electrician, and I headed over Snoqualmie Pass in the Cascade Mountains for Thorp, which was about a two hour drive by car. Nearing Thorp we spotted the engine and train on the mainline behind a farm house. The farmer let us drive through his pasture in order to get as close to the engine as we could.

17. Wheel Lathe. *Photo, Ed Eckes.*

RAIL TALES

I climbed through the fence and up the bank and onto the engine. We turned on the fuel pump and checked the fuel sight glasses for fuel. There was none in the suction or pressure glass. Checking further we found the fuel suction line at the fuel pump was hanging loose. I attached the fitting and tightened it, then turned on the fuel pump and watched as the fuel filled the sight glass. We started the engine and checked everything out. About that time the Road Foreman showed up and asked what was causing the trouble. When he found out, he lit into the engine crew for not looking for the trouble, as it was obvious what the problem was. Joe and I returned to Auburn about 7:00 p.m. — another easy road job.

In the late 1970s, one night, about midnight, the phone rang and it was the roundhouse foreman, Vic Ricci at Auburn. He said they had a mud slide at Eagle Gorge, located alongside the Green River in the Cascade Mountains. The pile driver had been sent up to help clean up the slide but it wasn't operating correctly. The pile driver operator couldn't get one traction motor in gear.

I said, "Can't you get somebody else to go up and work on it?"

Ricci said, "You are the only one around who has worked on the pile driver traction motor gear boxes, and you are needed up there."

I finally agreed to go and said I would need a helper to accompany me. So, Ricci called Ben Robertson and we met at the diesel house about 1:00 a.m. We picked up all the tools I thought we would need, put them in the company truck and headed for Kanaskat. At Kanaskat we were to be picked up by a speeder and taken to Eagle Gorge. It was pouring down rain when we arrived at Kanaskat forty minutes later and we waited for the speeder to show up. After it finally arrived, we loaded our tools on it and climbed on for the trip up the track. We bounced along over every joint in the track and the headlight seemed to point in all directions except the one in which we were headed. It was like going full speed into a black waterfall.

After a while, we could see some lights ahead and suddenly we were at the slide site. We climbed off the speeder and

11. Auburn Diesel House, October 5, 1945. *Courtesy Washington State Archives, Puget Sound Branch.*

walked alongside the work train to locate the foreman in charge. The foreman said to see the pile driver operator, so we headed on up the track. When we got up by the pile driver all we could see (even with the powerful flood lights), was a sea of mud. Ben suddenly sank down to his thighs in the mud and we grabbed each other and made our way back to higher ground. Later, we decided he must have stepped off the track ballast into the ditch.

The pile driver operator showed me which traction motor wouldn't go into gear. I told him I would have to crawl under the pile driver and open the inspection cover to check the gears inside. After seeing what the trouble was, then I could decide if it was something I could repair. He said he would try to divert the water and mud that was running over the top of the rails and under the pile driver.

The pile driver is a multi-use machine. Besides driving piling, it has a clamshell bucket that was being used to dig out mud and debris from the plugged culvert. It can also be used as a crane to lift rail and other heavy materials.

After a while, the operator diverted most of the mud and water, so I threw a couple of pieces of cardboard under the pile driver and crawled up to the traction motor case. I then started to remove the inspection cover. While under the pile driver, I began to think about what I would do if another slide came down the mountain. I could hear Green River roaring down below us on one side and we were between it and the unseen mountain on the other side. This was where the mud slide had come from and it could happen again. I thought I should get this over with and get out from under there.

After removing the inspection cover, I looked over all the gears and everything looked okay except the sliding gear, which was out to the end of its travel, and the screw threads were jammed. I had Ben and the operator put the crank in place and pull on the handle, while I pounded on the counterweight with a hammer. Suddenly it broke loose.

They were now able to get the gear cranked in place. I put the inspection cover back in place, crawled back out and headed back to the work train for some coffee and something to eat.

10. Auburn locomotive center, May 25, 1946. *Photo, Albert Farrow.*

The pile driver operator went back to clearing the slide. I never saw what this location looked like in daylight, but will never forget that night.

Ben and I got back to Auburn about daylight. This job could have been a lot worse than it turned out to be.

I went to work for the Northern Pacific Railway in July of 1942 at the age of sixteen. My first job was greasing locomotives, then I was a fire builder, machinist helper and fired yard switchers when they were short of firemen at Auburn Yard.

I joined the Navy in September 1943, and when I returned from the service I went back to work for the railroad in August 1946 as a machinist helper and then to machinist helper apprentice in August 1948. I was promoted to machinist on October 22, 1951. My service on the railroad was for about forty-three years with both the Northern Pacific and later Burlington Northern Railroads before retiring October 1, 1987.

Passenger connection train between Auburn and Tacoma in 1946. *Photo: Albert Farrow*

74. Mar Hebert, Conductor. *Mar Hebert Collection.*

MOUNTAIN BLIZZARD

By Mar Hebert- Auburn, Washington

One day in December in the early 1950s, just a few days before Christmas, we had a huge snowstorm in western Washington. The only mode of transportation was train travel as the buses and airlines were all down.

There was freezing weather on the mountain and the snowplows were working around the clock to keep the main line of the Northern Pacific Railway open between Lester and Easton, Washington through the Cascade Mountains. Passenger train No. 25 from the east was running as a passenger extra and was over twelve hours late. It had endured a hard time through Montana.

No. 2 out of Seattle to the east had orders telling us of the "run late," and we were permitted to reach Lester for the meet with the passenger extra. At Lester we pulled up to the depot to see if anything had changed. We heard we were definitely stuck at Lester for the other train.

We loaded on two section men and dropped them off at the switch to the House track. In order to pull our train off the main line into the clear, we were going to have to head in on the House track, which the snowplow hadn't had a chance to plow.

We backed down the main line and prepared to make "a run for it." When the section men got the switch dug out and lined, we were given a "highball" and chugged onto the House track. Thank God, the engineer was able to pull us just into the clear!

We knew we were going to be in for a wait in that little isolated, mountain town of Lester nestled in a deep valley in the Cascade Mountains. We didn't know then, but it would be for two long hours. In the meantime, we had the engineer cut the steam a little and retrieved blankets from the Pullman cars to help keep the passengers comfortable.

The passengers were not told of the severity of the storm or the seriousness of the situation. An added problem was conserving water. We dared not run out of it, as there was no way we could get water into the tank of the steam engine at Lester. The temperature was fourteen degrees below freezing.

73. Lester water tank in winter. *Photo, Dallas Barnard.*

72. Lester depot in 1949. *Photo, Dallas Barnard.*

RAIL TALES

The brakeman and I took turns walking through the coaches every so often to see that all was well with the passengers. They "bitched" and verbally attacked us every time we passed through. About ninety percent of them were disgruntled airline passengers who wouldn't have gotten home for Christmas without train transportation. They hated to travel by train and wanted us to know it by taking out their frustrations on us.

When the passenger extra finally went by, we were issued single track orders to proceed over the mountain to Easton. There was now a terrific blizzard raging in the mountains and we knew the going would be tough.

Starting out of Lester we thought the track would be clear because of the passenger extra just passing over it. We were wrong! The snow drifts had fallen in right behind the other train and we progressed slower than usual fighting our way through them.

We got through the first tunnel and just as we prepared to enter the long tunnel, we hit a huge snow drift which slowed us to three or four miles per hour. Luckily though, we pushed our way along and entered the two mile long Stampede Tunnel.

If we had stalled at that location, it would have been a terrible catastrophe to be trapped in the tunnel. We couldn't have backed down the track out of the tunnel because of the snow piling up on the tracks behind us. This sobering thought was continually with the crew as we worried about everybody and what our chances were. The area was in a remote mountain pass and there was no way for anybody to reach us. Help might possibly have been able to come from Easton, but that option was very slim.

We were reduced to praying that we could make it and the good Lord was certainly with us. Our prayers finally were answered though and we did! Railroading on the mountain could be a scary experience during the winter months each year and nobody with any sense took it lightly.

RAIL TALES

WORST ACCIDENT

By Joe LaPorte - Tacoma, Washington

My service dates on the railroad (Northern Pacific and Burlington Northern) were, January 23, 1942, until my retirement date on, March 4, 1986. I spent forty-five years on the railroad, and I think the worst accident that I've been in, was when I killed a boy at Sultan, Washington.

On June 8, 1973, I was on Burlington Northern train No. 81 from Wenatchee, Washington to Seattle, Washington with 114 cars. My speed was about fifty miles per hour when the accident occurred.

It was a pleasant day and the time was about 6:30 p.m. Brakeman Pat Lyman and I were talking about this and that when all of a sudden a car shot out of a private road. We hit the car right on the door post, on the passenger side.

The brakeman was standing up looking out the window and yelled a warning just before we hit. It was too late. I blew the whistle once and put the train into emergency. The boy flew out and the car just blew into pieces. It was a 1959, white Oldsmobile, Super 88.

The boy, sixteen years old, had just graduated and had been given the car as a gift. He was so excited about the car that he paid little attention to the rail crossing and evidently didn't hear us coming.

It's not necessary to whistle for these private crossings, unless there is a whistle sign. People who live near railroad tracks are knowledgeable about the possibility of a train coming, and usually look first before crossing a track.

In Sultan on highway No. 2 across the street, the state patrol and sheriff were at the local delicatessen when the accident occurred and were on the scene immediately to take charge.

The town of Sultan was tied up for three hours and the whole town was unhappy. The tragedy was bad enough, but there was a wedding that evening and half the party were on the other side of the tracks, with no way to get across.

In trying to get the train stopped, we pulled a drawbar and had to take the car to Monroe and set it out on a siding. Then we returned to pick up our train, which caused another two hour delay. Since there was no damage to the rail or ties, we finished the run. It was a bad day from start to the end.

64. The inside of an NP mail car – 1968. *Photo, Bud Emmons.*

LOCKED IN

By Sam Watterson - Enumclaw, Washington

During my fireman days on the Tacoma Division East of the Northern Pacific Railway, I remember firing for engineer Dave Norman in the late 1950s. I especially remember one morning going west on passenger train No. 25. Part of my job was to do a water inspection in the baggage car and in order to do this I had to climb through the nose of the diesel to reach the car behind. As I went through I unsnapped the bolts that locked the door shut, but didn't lock them. I just opened the door and went into the car and checked the water tank in the baggage car, but when I tried to return through the door to the engine — the door had slammed shut and locked.

BY GOD . . . I WAS STUCK IN THE BAGGAGE CAR!

I was afraid Dave would start to worry about me after a while, so when we went through Cle Elum I dropped off a message that I was locked in the car. When the amused operator advised the dispatchers of the problem, they choked with laughter and right away thought Dave didn't want me riding in the engine with him.

By the time we got to Easton (the next station west of Cle Elum) Dave was concerned enough about my whereabouts to stop the train, and rescued me from the baggage car. We came the rest of the way to Seattle without any more problems.

From then on I made sure those doors were locked in place before I did this part of my job. The picture of the incident is stamped in my head as it was an embarrassing moment, to tell the truth! There I was, the fireman on the passenger train standing in the doorway of the baggage car coming into Easton when I should have been on the engine. This was a kind of happening a railroader never lives down!

HEY! WHAT HAPPENED?

By Dallas Barnard - Kirkland, Washington

In 1948, I finished some military training in California and was being transferred along with other members of my unit to Camp Crowder, Missouri. I was given sixteen days to make the trip from one military base to the other. This is what the army called a delay enroute. That apparently was a more acceptable term than a wartime furlough. So, I decided to spend some time with my family in Auburn, Washington.

I had a great time visiting my parents and younger brother Ken and at the same time learned a few things about the state of Washington. I learned the only watering holes were taverns where you could buy beer and wine but not a mixed drink. If you wanted something stronger you visited the state owned liquor store and purchased a bottle of concentrated spirits and took it elsewhere else to sample it. If you wanted a drink out of your own bottle, you visited what was known as a "Private Club," where you were charged an exorbitant admission fee to be able to mix your own liquor with the mix of your choice, supplied by the club at some equally exorbitant price.

Coming from California this was quite an education for me. In the first place, I didn't know the state of Washington was in the liquor business. I just couldn't imagine a bunch of bureaucrats who probably couldn't even tie their own shoes, being in the liquor business of selling a product like this, when the only knowledge they had of the business was that the stuff tasted good. They may have also known if they drank enough of it would allow them to forget that they were supposed to be representing the people who paid their exorbitant salaries.

My vacation over, I boarded a Northern Pacific Railway train in Auburn sometime in the evening headed for Portland, Oregon. When I boarded the train, I knew there was a possibility of a delay on the way due to a freight train derailment somewhere down the line. I had no idea where that was, but I was assured, however, that I would be able to make my connection in Portland, Oregon for points east.

RAIL TALES

It was daylight when the train eased to a stop somewhere in southern Washington. I had no idea where we were, but the conductor told us we were near Castle Rock. There didn't appear to be a depot in the vicinity and soon the conductor came through and told everyone that we were at the scene of the previous wreck. He told us that there would be a delay until work on the rails was completed and we could be on our way. So, many of us got off the train and walked up past the locomotive to the wreck site. The workmen were spiking rails down, and finally the crane went back and forth across the repaired section a couple of times to make sure it was all right. About then the conductor came along and told everyone to get back on the train because we would be leaving soon.

We were getting nicely settled in our seats again, ready to resume our journey. I had leaned back in my coach seat hoping that I could maybe catch a couple of winks before we got to Portland when I felt something hit me in the back of the head, and I was thrown forward into the seat in front of me. At the same time I heard glass breaking and stuff falling off the overhead rack. In a couple of seats ahead of me, there was a lady with two little girls. I realized that was where one of the windows was broken. There was broken glass all over the two little girls and covering the seat.

We got the broken glass off the children and moved the family to a vacant seat and then a group of us got off the train to see what had happened. Walking to the rear of our train we saw another locomotive had rammed into the rear of the train we were riding on, and the tender looked as though it was trying to climb over the locomotive. After examining this new wreckage, we saw a man from that train also taking a look. From all his newspaper pictures, we all realized that this was Thomas E. Dewey and this was his campaign train. Of course he was unhurt and just out surveying to see what was interfering with his campaign plans.

We never did find out why his engineer wasn't aware that our train was on that track and that this was only a single line and there would be no passing. My own opinion was that the locomotive was being run by a Republican bureaucrat and all decisions were made by committee. When it came time to read a signal or make a decision they had to take a vote first.

Now, the railroad really had trouble — the original wreck and then two more trains suffering with problems. It began to look like overtime was piling up for section crews and everyone else involved with this new cleanup operation.

The passengers on our train consisted mostly of servicemen and their families. And, of course, during wartime there were the ever present military police. These were the young servicemen who swaggered around with their armbands, night sticks and large caliber revolvers, trying to look important.

This dilemma was deepening and the question was what were they going to do with all of the servicemen and their families on this train? Soon, a couple of ambulances came along and removed the injured people from the rear coach of the train. Fortunately, no one was seriously injured, just a few sprains and some cuts and bruises.

After sitting around for about an hour, all the servicemen were ordered off the train by the Military Police. We were told that someone had contacted Vancouver Barracks and they were sending transportation for us to get to Portland. The weather had been merely overcast until that time and now it started with a typical Washington rain. About a quarter of a mile away was a highway overpass. All of us who had been ordered off the train by the Military Police (in their infinite wisdom) were soon huddled under this overpass and feeling miserable.

The train hadn't been moved, but the Army felt it was better for us to huddle under the overpass than sit down and wait on the train. After about two hours of this, our transportation arrived. It consisted of a convoy of large Army trucks with canvas covers over the back.

The modern-day covered wagon! All the servicemen and families piled into the back of these trucks and rode the rest of the way to Portland. This was not riding in the lap of luxury. There was no heat and there were hard wooden slats they called seats in a vehicle designed to work in a rock quarry.

We finally arrived in the Portland railroad station and exited the trucks in search of warmth and a decent meal. We were told that the train leaving Portland would be delayed until further notice so we had dinner in the station. After a hot meal we headed for our train to find a seat.

Boarding the train, we located a conductor who appeared to know what was going on, and he informed us they were waiting for the train that had been rear-ended, so that those passengers could make a connection.

I'm sure we would have had a much more comfortable ride on that train, broken windows and all, than we had on those quarry trucks. Of course the Army knew what was best for us I'm sure, and the rest of the trip was uneventful. This may give you an idea of life in the '40s from those of us who lived it.

HELPER SERVICE

By Joe LaPorte - Tacoma, Washington

Danger to a railroad man can come in many ways, even sometimes when you are getting help.

It happened late that Friday morning on October 5, 1979, when a west bound freight was over tonnage and needed some help on the Chumstick Hill near Leavenworth, Washington.

When Burlington Northern Conductor Scalf on the freight train asked for some help, he got more than he bargained for. Engineer Kirby on the helper engine came up over the hill on a curve and before he knew it, found the rear end of the freight train right in front of him . . . and they hit! It derailed the caboose and one box car.

The mishap shook up the crew and probably surprised them a bit. There were no serious injuries reported.

NP RCU-1. Picture taken at Livingston, Montana, Sept. 2, 1972.
Photo J.M. Fredrickson.

RAIL TALES

SLAVES

By Blackie Moser - Auburn, Washington

Early in 1968, the Northern Pacific brought something new to our Tacoma Division. This was when the remote controlled slave units arrived.

These amounted to radio controlled helper units. Each set had a "Master," on the head end that contained the radio control. Back in the train was the slave. It was a unit with receiving and deciphering controls, bossing two or three other units coupled to it. This was to provide power to pull bigger trains over our mountain territory without concentrating too much tractive effort on the head end. Before they left, they were going to make some of our lives a great deal more exciting!

Training seminars were held on the operation of these units and the technical aspects of them. Your qualifications to run them could only be obtained by attending several of these classes, then making three trips accompanied by the Road Foreman of Engines.

I attended the classes as quickly as I could. I thought at first that this was the coming thing in train handling, and I wanted the qualification. I had received my "OK" as an engineer in chain gang several months before this time. Because a number of men on the engineers' extra board were not qualified on the mountain district, I was often used out of turn as an engineer over the hill.

At this time I was holding a chain gang turn with Harry Iverson. With his help in convincing the road foreman to ride with us, I soon received my qualification.

I continued to fire for him through the spring and on into summer, until the trip before his retirement on August 25, 1968. Looking back in my old time book I see that we had the slaves eleven times and I was used alone as engineer on them four times.

A very bad reputation was beginning to surround these machines. They seemed to occasionally develop a mind of their own. The results were not good. Radio communication, essential to their operation would be lost between them. At times, such as going through Stampede Tunnel, the reason would be apparent. At other times there would be no discernible cause. According to "Hoyle," when continuity was lost, after twenty seconds, the slaves went into idle, the air brake functions were 'cut out', and they became as inert as boxcars. It sounded very good in theory, but reality was far different.

I believe the first ones to have serious trouble were Engineer Frank Possolo and Conductor Jack Osborne. Let me set the scene:

The Stampede Tunnel is almost exactly two miles long. It is a steep grade up to each end of it, and the crest is almost exactly in the center. The grades once you enter the mouths of the tunnel become less severe. From the east to the crest is two tenths of one percent, and from the west to the crest is seven tenths of one percent. To finish the picture, at the west mouth is a ten degree curve.

Frank had a dead freight west. For power he had three lead units and four slave units. Loaded to the limit, he went into the east end of the "hole" perhaps at ten miles per hour. Almost at once, the light came on telling him that he had lost continuity with the slave units. As the speed began to pick up on the diminishing grade, he eased off on his head end power. He was confident that the slaves would drop out in twenty seconds and he would pull the train through after that with the lead units. By the time the train reached the speed limit of twenty miles per hour and he had shut the throttle completely off, it was apparent something was seriously wrong.

Over the crest of the tunnel he was gaining speed at an alarming rate. He had placed the lead units in dynamic brake and attempted to set the air brakes. Dynamic brakes are a means of converting the traction motors of a diesel unit to a generator. Then, by employing suitable resistance, they become brakes to retard the train speed. The slave units having failed to drop out, were still shoving full throttle, negating any attempt at controlling the train.

RAIL TALES

He came out of the tunnel mouth very fast and into the ten degree curve. Surprisingly enough, the lead engine and cars made it without derailing. The slaves emerged from the tunnel. Radio contact was again restored and the result was disaster. Immediately the slaves shut down, and went into full dynamic brake, just as the train brakes went into emergency. Eight cars of corn and three cars of lumber were on their side! Three more derailed, the siding was torn out, and the head-end was a mile down the mountain before it stopped.

No one was hurt this time, but there were some very frightened men. There was a good deal of finger pointing and buck passing, but nothing was really resolved. The company, without directly saying so or issuing discipline, let us know how they felt. It was human error. On our part, we did not yet know enough about the machines to counter that claim.

Very shortly thereafter, the next incident befell Homer McElreath and a conductor whose name is not at hand. The occurrence was almost the same as the previous one, except no derailment. After a wild four mile ride, the train finally came to a halt with most of the brake shoes burned completely off. Disillusionment was setting in.

The next incident could have been hilarious were it not for the portent of disaster that it contained. A long drag of empties made it successfully over the mountain. The crew changed at Yakima and the train continued on to Toppenish where there was some switching to be done. The engineer went through all the proper procedures to ensure that the slaves were disabled before cutting the head end power away. Once satisfied that all was well, they went about the task at hand.

Their switching took them out of sight of the rear of the train, so it was not at once apparent that the slaves had come back to life on their own. They had released the brakes on the train, and were responding to every throttle command being made. The first inkling of trouble was the rear end of the train suddenly appearing and ramming into the side of the cars they were shoving into an industry. Again, no one hurt, but no real solution surfaced as to what happened, or how to prevent it from reoccurring.

Suddenly it was Jack Osborne's turn again, and this time with a vengeance. I will let him tell it in his own words. The following is the exact text of the accident report he filed:

I had my full rest and went on duty at Auburn as conductor on Train 606. I think we were called for 8:00 a.m., May 18, 1968. The rear brakeman was W. M. Bauer. E. D. Rice was head brakeman, and he was on the engine. Engineer Willard and Fireman Rodifer were on the engine with Road Foreman Jack Wynn. This was the entire crew."

We had three units on the head end and three slave units were cut in at about forty percent of the tonnage from the rear end. We had sixty-four loads, forty-one empties and 5514 tons. We were running eastward to Yakima. Air was in the train line, pressure was normal, and the brakes operated properly when we came down the hill. We did not make many stops.

I was sitting in the cupola of our caboose, number 1105, on the north side, or left side facing the direction of movement. Bauer was on the right side of the cupola, and we were maintaining sharp lookouts. Everything was fine coming into Thorp. (The conductor's sir valve is positioned ahead of the seat in the center of the cupola. This valve flips sideways when you dump the air or place it in emergency.)

We were running at sixty miles per hour, which was determined by Road Foreman Wynn, when the head end came to the east switch of the westward siding. Wynn immediately called Ellensburg by radio to have someone look at the switch as there was a bad sun kink in the switch. To my knowledge, the head end did not then attempt to reduce speed.

When he said that, I stuck my head out the window and looked forward. I could see the cars whipping through the switch.

I hollered to Bauer, "I don't think we are going to make it," and immediately tried to pull the air.

Instead of the explosion that would have told me the brakes were in emergency, there was only a prolonged blow from the valve. At that time, I saw what looked like the third car from the caboose go on the ground. I tried to get back in my seat and hollered to Bauer to hang on as we were on the ground.

About that time Bauer said, "We're going over!"

The caboose broke off the end of the rear of the train and fell over to the right on the ground in the ditch. I knew I was falling, and when the caboose came to rest, I was beside Bauer on the right cupola side of the caboose.

Jack was severely injured with a fracture of the first lumbar vertebra, which has troubled him badly for years. While the slaves in this incident did not cause the accident, the inability of the conductor to place the brakes in emergency certainly worsened the damage.

With the rear three cars and caboose broken off, the rest of the train still did not go into emergency as it should have. It, in fact, continued on until Jack was able to pickup the caboose radio and advise the head end crew what had occurred. It was over three miles before a stop was effected.

Again no real explanation of how this could happen was forthcoming. The Radar Corporation that manufactured the radio controls made several modifications and assured us the problem was solved.

From the time the slaves first came until Harry's retirement, my experiences with them, with one exception, were very good. Even that small exception was not truly a malfunction and turned out to be funny. How funny depended on your point of view.

May 29, Harry Iverson laid off for a trip. His turn was caught by Dave Benson. We were called for Train 606 on duty at Auburn, Washington at 7:30. It was a beautiful early summer morning.

At this time, Dave had not yet received his "OK" on the slaves. The crew caller, on seeing who stood for the trip, notified Road Foreman Glen Staeheli, and was advised to go ahead and call him. It was his intent, he said, to ride with us, and if all went well, to give Dave his qualification.

Everything went very well. We went to the yard and doubled our train together. That is to say that it was on two tracks, and we pulled one and put it to the other. We performed the required tests and started out. By the time we reached the town of Lester, sixty miles to the east, Glen was convinced Dave would be okay for service, He was so convinced of this in fact that he opted to ride the slave units over the mountain and through the tunnel. He wanted to see first hand how they were performing.

It is ten miles from Lester to the mouth of the Stampede Tunnel. At the time it was double track. One track for eastbound and one for westbound traffic. It lies on a 2.2 grade. This means that it rises 2.2 tenths feet in height for each one-hundred feet of track. While this is not much to an automobile or a person walking, it is very stiff for a freight train.

Just short of the tunnel we met a westbound train. We knew at once the smoke in the hole would be bad. Because the crest of the hill was in the middle of the tunnel, it had no natural draught. There was a ventilating plant at the west end, but it was woefully inadequate to clear the bore quickly. We nosed our train into the tunnel, and our worst fears were realized. The smoke and heat from the preceding train seemed practically solid.

Just before the crest of the hill the no continuity light came on telling us radio contact with the slaves had been lost. This time instead of the slaves pushing us out of the tunnel, the reverse was true. In twenty seconds they were inert. The air brake control dropped out, and because our train was extremely long, the air brakes began to set up on the rear end.

Dave worked power, then more power. It became apparent that to continue to do so would break the train in two. Finally we stalled. The head-end was just short of the mouth of the hole, and the slaves were just about at the high point of the tunnel. This was the hottest, smokiest spot, and they contained the road foreman.

Glen Staeheli was a big man, a very big man. The clearance between the tunnel walls and the engine was small, and there was no way that he was going to get out unless we got the train outside. Dave asked if I had any ideas. I suggested that we place the brakes in emergency, then after ninety seconds release them. It was my idea that then, even with the slaves not working, the brakes on the entire train would equalize and release. This we did, and for once an idea paid off. Waiting an ample time for them to release, Dave applied power and we rolled easily down the hill.

The engines were so covered with soot and smoke, we had to open the side windows and stick our heads out to see. There was no way that we could see the slaves, but we knew what they must look like.

We finally reached Cle Elum and stopped to do our station work. Glen walked up from the units while we were working and climbed up on the head end. I turned and looked at him and it took every bit of will power I had to keep from breaking out in hysterical laughter. There was no way to tell what color his clothes had ever been. His shirt was wringing wet from sweat. The only white parts of his face were his teeth and eyes. Where he had rubbed his hands over his face, the soot had taken on a shine like shoe polish.

Without saying a word, he picked up the water jug out of the ice bucket and drank about a quart. Finally, he put the jug down and looked at Dave and me.

Then he asked, "Which one of you had the idea of putting the train into emergency?"

I was unsure of what mood he was in, but reluctantly admitted that it was my idea.

He looked at me for a few moments, then said, "I think you probably saved my life. Anyway, it's worth whatever you want for dinner when we get to Yakima."

He was as good as his word.

The day before Harry Iverson retired, I was set up running. I worked the extra board out of Auburn, and was demoted on the eleventh of November. I went back firing chain gang this time for a man named Jim Colson.

I did not know then that Jim was terminally ill with brain cancer. He had never exactly been a stable person, but even for him, his behavior was unusual. Looking back now in retrospect, it is not surprising. He had me doing almost all the running. Most of the time he was very withdrawn. I am now sure that must have been from pain and medication.

On December 15, we were called for Train 640 at 12:45 p.m. The conductor was Jack Osborn, the rear brakeman,

Bruce Ray, and the head brakeman was Pete Deede. Our train consisted of forty loads, one hundred twenty-two empties and weighed seven thousand plus tons. For power we had three high horse power units on the head end and four units cut in sixty tow cars deep.

I can't say that I had any sort of premonition, but never before was I as fussy with the car inspectors or as particular with the brake tests. A point that later came up many times. About 3:00 p.m. we left the yard and started east.

It had been a dreary day when we started out of Auburn, and when we came out of the east end of Stampede Tunnel, it was snowing heavily. When we reached the bottom of the hill, there were several inches of new snow and it was blowing badly. Visibility was very poor.

At Easton we picked up an order instructing us (because of our extreme length) to head into the westward siding and pull through into the eastward siding at Cle Elum to meet train 601

It is thirteen miles between Easton and Cle Elum. The track lies on a slight down hill grade all the way. Halfway between the two points was a siding called Nelson. There was a sixty mile an hour curve here while the rest of the track was seventy-five. Nelson siding was where the drama began.

Approaching Nelson, I was running about sixty-seven miles per hour. About a mile from the curve I set some brakes to get down to the required sixty. I was working enough power at the time to keep the train stretched. I released the brakes and could see that I was going to get down just a bit slower than I wanted to. I reached up and opened the throttle from four to five and glanced at the slave console as I did so. I watched the slaves go from number four throttle position to number eight throttle which is wide open. This phenomenon occurred often, and as they usually dropped back to five in just a few seconds, it was not a matter of concern. However, as I was watching, the dreaded no continuity light appeared.

While I was still pondering the ramifications of this development, the slack was driven violently in against the lead units. Indeed, the slaves were in full throttle. I responded by attempting to set the brakes in the normal manner. It was no more effective than normal brakes had been. I got no emergency brakes behind the slaves and perhaps on only half the cars on the head end. Ninety seconds and two miles later, the air from the slave units released even those.

By this time the speedometer had run up off the top of the scale. The over speed whistle was screaming. Air was roaring out of the emergency port from the slave units. Two other men in the cab were screaming at me to do something, and I had discovered what the true meaning of fear was! I knew that there was a train on the main line that we had to meet at Cle Elum. I did not know if they were there yet, but I did know that I had passed the point where I could possibly stop short of the siding I was to head into.

In those days, our engines had radios, but very few, if any of the cabooses had been equipped with them yet. I was calling on the radio, trying to warn the other crew on the other engine at Cle Elum that we were running away, and to stop and get clear if they could of our train. The snow was blowing heavily and the crew in the caboose were so covered with it that they had no idea where they were or how fast we were really going.

Finally, Bruce Ray started to sense something was amiss. He dug into his grip and came out with one of the first company portable radios we had. He poked the antenna out the window and the most blessed words I ever heard were, "Blackie is something wrong?"

All I could say was, "Plug her Bruce, for God's sake plug her!"

He reached over and grabbed the emergency valve in the caboose, and that was the final bit needed. The slaves finally tripped, shut down, and the train went into emergency. We roared around the last curve and into a rock cut at the west end of Cle Elum at what was estimated later at over a hundred miles an hour.

At this point, I still had heard nothing from the opposing train. At least, though, he was not standing on the main line at the west end of the siding. We tore down the 7800 foot siding into the twenty-five mile an hour curve by the depot. It was still fast enough to move the track out of line, but we were slowing down. We finally came to a halt just clear of the siding switch at the east end of the yard.

After a long, stunned silence, we started to assess our situation. Minutes later, Bud Garret, the engineer on the train we were to have met called to find out if we got stopped.

We found out afterward that when they heard me call that we were running away he simply went into emergency. When their train stopped, they got away from the right of way. Finally, after what they were sure had been long enough for me to get there if we were still moving, they ventured back and called on the radio. We were able to contact the caboose again and found they had stopped west of west siding switch. From this we knew our train was broken in two at least once. In fact, it turned out to be broken in four places.

The westbound arrived and I hitched a ride with them to the slave units. I pulled jumper cables, fuses, switches and anything else I thought made them run. When I finished, they were inert iron.

With the help of the westbound, we replaced the couplers that were broken, coupled up the various pieces of the train and finally started on to Yakima. The rest of the trip was long and slow, only having power on the head end, but without further incident.

The fun was just starting. We had telephoned the dispatcher and had given him a brief synopsis of what had happened at Cle Elum. When we got to Yakima, we filed a message describing the incident to the master mechanic and the superintendent, The slaves went east to Spokane as dead iron. There, every official within range descended on them determined to prove again that it was human error.

Our trip home was uneventful with the exception that Jim Colson was physically ill all the way. We got to Auburn, put the train away and came back to the yard office. At that point, he simply went home, leaving me to take the engine to the roundhouse. There, was the reception committee primed and ready. After first wanting to know why Jim was not with me, and sending someone to his home to determine that he was ill and not drunk, the interrogation started. It went on for over two hours. Finally, everyone seemed to run out of questions and I was allowed to register in and go home.

Another trip followed with no slaves and an extra board engineer. Upon arrival back at Auburn, I found I was promoted again, and there would be a formal hearing on the incident four days hence. I was to arrange to have whatever representation I wished to present. We were not charged with any rule or operating practice violation.

The formal hearing was quite a gathering. The company had all its principal mechanical officers there. Each craft had at least two of its representatives there plus a regional vice president from the Locomotive Engineers. The Radar Corporation, manufacturer of the equipment, flew in personnel, and the stage was set.

Jess Cannon, Chief Mechanical Officer for the Northern Pacific, opened the meeting with a statement that I have never forgotten.

He said, "Let's understand at the start that we are not here to hang anyone for this. We are here to find out what happened, and why!"

Everyone that had even a remote part in the trip was questioned at great length. As I had been running the locomotive, I received what I considered more than a fair share of the attention. Finally about five that evening all the relevant ground had been covered, so they dropped the other shoe. They had assembled a test train in the yard with the slaves. It was as close a duplicate to the one we had run as they could make it. I was called to run it, and Jack Osborne and his men were the train crew.

The whole assembly moved to the yard plus a new collection of experts. They filled the cab of the lead locomotive and streamed out onto the running boards and the ground. For over four hours, they set up various tests. Out of these, five different times, they created conditions under which the train would not go into emergency.

Finally their testing completed, Master Mechanic Moreau said, "Well, I guess we are done. You can leave town now."

I was stunned. They had proved that conditions could happen where I could not control the train; a fact I already well knew. Now I was supposed to leave town?

At this point, Road Foreman Bob Stewart endeared himself to me then and forever.

He looked out over the backs of the retreating experts from the cab window and roared, "Wait a minute! Aren't any of you SONS OF BITCHES going to ride with this man?"

They all looked at one another, collectively shrugged and continued to walk away.

Bob said, "Blackie, don't move. I'm going to get my suitcase and go with you."

He was as good as his word. In a short while he was back, and we were on our way. The trip over the mountain was uneventful until we got to Cle Elum again.

This time, we had one car behind the engine to set out. We came in and stopped, made sure the slaves were cut out and dead, then cut the engine away from the train. The switch was filled with snow, so it took some while to get it dug out and ready to use. Bob was sitting on the fireman's side relaxed.

I was leaning out the cab window looking for a signal when the radio came on and said, "The air is releasing on the caboose, and the caboose is moving."

As I turned to grab the radio, a glance at the control panel confirmed my worst fears. The slaves had come to life by themselves, and they were releasing the brakes on the train. Bob got on the radio ahead of me and told the rear end to put the train in emergency, which they did. Bob was a wild man.

"Never mind setting out the car, put the train back together and don't move till I get back."

He walked back to the slaves and did the same surgery I had the week previously. When he got back, we went on to Yakima and the slaves were again just cold iron.

That was the end of them for us on the Northern Pacific. Time passed, the Northern Pacific became part of the Burlington Northern, I was set up running the year around, Bob Stewart went other places, then in 1977 he came back to us as Master Mechanic. Not too much later, the slaves reappeared.

At one of the first training seminars, I was sitting in the front row, and Bob came in to conduct the class. I guess the look on my face must have betrayed how I felt.

Bob looked at me for a moment, and said, "Don't start with me, this time they are going to work."

There is no need to relate all the misery and expense caused before they were finally removed from here permanently. Bob and I bumped into each other just after that in the roundhouse as I was leaving for work. I opened my mouth to say hello.

He stopped me with, "Whatever you are going to say about the slaves, I just don't want to hear it."

With that, he turned and walked away.

Last BN passenger train for Portland before Amtrack, April 30, 1971. *Photo: Bud Emmons*

Boomer telegrapher and dispatcher, Norman C. Peterson, left, with his friend Dave Sprau, at a gathering of former NP employees in July 1993, wherein Sprau introduced Pete as "A Legendary figure." Peterson died shortly afterward, a suspected casualty of the hard lifestyle extemporaneously attributed him in story and legend. *Photo, Dave Sprau.*

RAIL TALES

LIKE THIS?

By Dave Sprau - Ravensdale, Washington

Most everyone thinks of me as a telegrapher and train dispatcher, but it "ain't necessarily so." Let me tell you about an interlude in the usual course of my railroad career.

In June of 1969 I was working as a locomotive fireman on the Cascade Division of the Great Northern Railway. I managed to mark up on a vacancy in the Skykomish - Cashmere helper pool with Engineer Wayne Williams and Conductor Roy Austin. We could be called at all indecent hours of the night and day to either run "light engine" from Skykomish to Cashmere and help a westward freight train, or else we would help an eastbound freight to Cashmere. We would then either run light or help a westbound back to Skykomish.

The usual result of this regimen was that we had considerable time to kill in Cashmere. The depot at Cashmere was manned at the time by an agent, Archie Crawford, a day operator, Wayne Hudson, and a second trick operator, Jim Gates. Jim had come to the Great Northern from one of the Canadian roads and was an excellent Morse man. I don't think he was too delighted at having to work second trick for someone else, as the greater share of his earlier career with the Great Northern had been as an agent at the now-closed station at Monitor, Washington, just west of Wenatchee.

Anyway, Jim tolerated helper crews killing time inside the Cashmere depot, but just barely. I am sure that as far as he was concerned I was just another trainman with bleary eyes and greasy overalls. Besides that, I was only twenty-five years old and probably looked more like eighteen.

One evening I returned from lunch uptown by myself, instead of in the company of the conductor and engineer. The office door was open and I invited myself in, as trainmen often do. Jim didn't mind as he was sitting at a back desk doing demurrage and the chair at the telegraph desk was unoccupied. Jim beckoned me to sit in it. Realizing he was busy, I occupied myself by reading a magazine.

The silence was soon broken by the telegraph sounder; "OM, OM, OM, F," it called once, then again.

Gates grumbled under his breath, "Damn it."

I feigned ignorance. "What's the matter?"

"Every time I get busy that damn relay office starts calling. I wish you trainmen knew how to telegraph so you could make yourselves useful!"

Again I feigned ignorance.

"It probably isn't too hard. What do you do, just open up that key and answer?"

Jim laughed.

"Yes, and then try to keep up with the sender."

"Like this?" I asked as I opened the key.

Jim's eyes grew big, and he looked kind of annoyed. Before he could say or do anything else, I tapped out "I, I, OM," closed the key, stuck a telegram blank in the mill and started copying as Seattle operator Larry Crawford ripped out a couple of telegrams. Fortunately, Larry was a good sender. I didn't have to break.

When he finished, I asked Jim, "What do you sign?"

That was twenty-three years ago and I have forgotten what he answered, but I think it was "G". Anyway I okayed the two messages and closed the key. By this time, Mr. Gates knew he'd been had.

"Where did you learn to do that?"

I had to tell him I had just come from the Northern Pacific, a "previous life" in which the last nine years had been spent as a telegrapher and train dispatcher. By now, he was enjoying my little joke. We had, as the line in the story by Edgar Allen Poe goes, "Many a laugh about it afterwards."

RAIL TALES

WHAT HAPPENED?

By Cliff Bendiksen - Tacoma, Washington

I was called as engineer on Burlington Northern Train 138 out of Portland, Oregon on October 8, 1977. We had a big train, but had set out a bunch of cars at Tacoma and another bunch at Auburn, so we were down to about thirty-nine cars and headed for Seattle, Washington. We had come out of Portland with six locomotive units and we set two of our units from the middle of the train on a side track at South Seattle for a southbound train to pick up.

I remember we stopped at the switch to make our crossover and I went back to cut the units apart. We had to run the head units up the track and then come back to get the middle two units and then across to the other track (the side track). Coming back, we coupled the head-end and the rest of the train together.

While I prepared to start back my brakeman lined the switches across. At this time I was standing between the units trying to uncouple them, but having difficulty because the angle cock was really stiff. I couldn't pull it with one hand, so I put my left foot in the middle of the drawbar and gave a pull with both hands.

Suddenly, there was a big bang accompanied by a crashing noise and I became airborne. As I sailed through the air I could see all of my consist; the units were going backward and metal pieces, including handrails and steps, were flying through the air. I thought even before I lit, *HOLY MACKEREL — WHAT HAPPENED?*

I was thrown about fifteen feet into the air, and twenty feet from the northbound track, clear over the southbound track and into the blackberry vines, landing on my right hip. About the time I was trying to untangle myself from the blackberry vines I heard a big boom, like a cannon. I looked up, and there was a sheet of flames blazing into the air.

Glancing around for my brakeman, I saw him quietly standing nearby. In a daze we both saw the engine was tipped over and burning from one end to the other. It had blown up!

167

Cliff Bendiksen, retired.

My brakeman continued to stand motionless, as if in shock, and looked blankly at the scene before us.

I said, "Did anybody get out of those units?"

He said, "No."

"We had better see if we can get them out," I shouted.

When we went over to them we saw the cab was split away from the engine and two guys were trapped inside. We were extremely afraid for them. The flames were licking at their feet and they were trapped in the engine that had turned over. We got the brakeman out first, but it wasn't easy as he was wearing boots and his foot was wedged in, making it impossible for us to free him. He finally unlaced his boot and pulled his foot free, and then we were able to pull him out.

Next we pulled out Dick Arnold, the engineer of the train that hit us. Both were burned, beat up and splattered with oil. Somebody called the fire department. We were so thankful they showed up right away.

When the fire engines pulled away, we finally began to piece it all together. It seems our brakeman lined the switch across and then ran back to help me, hoping to save some time. He didn't stay to protect the switch as dictated by the rule book.

Dick Arnold, engineer on Train 143, claimed he got by the last block and it was green. He came full blast and all of a sudden dived through the crossover and hit us head on. No one was killed, but I don't think Arnold's conductor ever worked again. Their train consisted of four diesel units and a caboose. When they hit, those guys in the caboose flew around like rubber balls. Later, seeing pictures of the caboose made me wonder how any of them could have survived.

Conductor Gallion on Train 143 injured his back. I got a few scratches and a bruise on my right hip after flying through the air and landing so hard. Engineer Arnold was unable to attend the investigation on November 14, 1977, so it was recessed until January 27, 1978, giving Arnold time to sufficiently recover from personal injuries.

The brakeman on our Train 138 was continually grilled about compliance with Rule 104B, and Rule 93 which concerned protecting his switch in making a crossover

82. Trains 143 and 138 collided October 9, 1977 at 5:15 a.m. *Photo, Jack Flagg.*

L116014 0020 0606 10/09/77 U985
TASK ZZ FROM R116031 VIA N274 BY NCH

TAF739 KY TACOMA OCT 9 515A

JJB RLG RET RWP DFB BTA HFP AFT JED RKM WBJ ST PAUL BNI-11
RAB JWW SBM CCM JES HML WCB DFP SEATTLE SEY-8
DHB EHN R W STEWART GWF WJG LDA CAK RFK TJS JAL RVM GWC RVR
R W SAXWOLD SEATTLE SEA-14
GAH VJR AUBURN AUG-2
CMW WRG PWA AUBURN AUC-3
TWB LIM CREW CALLERS BALMER SER-3
AEH AKD GGR JJS C AND E 3RD SD WORK EXTRA CENTRALIA CEE-6

AT 1145PM OCT 8 1977, HEAD BRAKEMAN NO 138 CONDR TAYLOR
ENGR BENDIKSEN UNITS 2510 WP 3007 WP 3060 WP 3062 WP 3012 2227
HAD LINED FACING POINT CROSSOVER WEST END OF SOUTH SEATTLE AT
MP 8.8 PACIFIC DIVN, THIRD SUBDIVN WHEN NO 143 CONDR GALLION
ENGR ARNOLD, UNITS 730 1630 707 720 APPROACHING AT
ESTIMATED SPEED OF 50 MPH RAN THRU CROSSOVER FROM WESTWARD
TO EASTWARD TRACK COLLIDING WITH NO 138

NO 143 WAS CABOOSE HOP, NO 138 HAD 24-9-2072
COLLISION RESULTED IN FOLLOWING DAMAGE AND PERSONAL INJURY
NO 143
UNIT 730 ON SIDE AND DESTROYED BY FIRE AND COLLISION
UNIT 1630 UPRIGHT DERAILED ON EASTWARD TRACK DESTROYED
UNIT 707 UPRIGHT DERAILED ON EASTWARD TRACK, SOME DAMAGE
UNIT 720 UPRIGHT DERAILED ON EASTWARD TRACK WITH PORTION OF UNIT
IN CROSSOVER NO APPARENT DAMAGE
CABOOSE REMAINED ON RAIL STOPPED IN CROSSOVER NO DAMAGE

NO 138
UNIT 2510 UPRIGHT, DERAILED AND DESTROYED
UNIT WP 3007 UPRIGHT DERAILED AND DESTROYED
WP 3060 WP 3062 WP 3010 BN 2227 REMAINED ON TRACK WITH
UNDETERMINED DAMAGE
HEAD FOUR CARS NO 138 SUSTAINED FOLLOWING DAMAGE
WP 11630 MTY SIDE BLOCKING EASTWARD AND PC MAIN LINES
$18,000 DAMAGE
WP 68143 PASTA, ON SIDE BLOCKING WESTWARD TRACK, $5500 DAMAGE
WP 68259 DETERGENT ON SIDE BLOCKING EASTWARD AND PC MAIN LINES
DESTROYED
WP 62099 DETERGENT UPRIGHT DERAILED ON EASTWARD TRACK
$1500 DAMAGE

PERSONAL INJURIES
ENGR ARNOLD SUFFERED BROKEN JAW, FRACTURED ANKLE, COMPOUND
FRACTURE ON OPPOSITE LEG
BRAKEMAN RAY SUFFERED HEAD LACERATIONS, SINGED FACE AND POSSIBLE
INTERNAL LUNG BURNS, BOTH REMOVED TO VALLEY GENERAL HOSPITAL
AUBURN WASH.
NOW EXPECT WESTWARD MAIN TRACK TO BE OPEN AT 700AM
EXTENSIVE DAMAGE TO EASTWARD TRACK
BALMER AND AUBURN DERRICKS CALLED ON DUTY IMMEDIATELY TO CLEAR
DERAILMENT. AUBURN-EVERETT TIME FRT TIED UP AT BALMER AND CREW
TRANSPORTED TO AUBURN BY TAXI. CREW 10 TIED UP AT SOUTH SEATTLE
AND CREW TRANSPORTED TO AUBURN BY TAXI. AUBURN DERRICK HANDLED
REAR OF NO 138,S TRAIN INTO CLEAR AT ORILLIA. CREW 4 WILL BE
HELD AT AUBURN FOR FURTHER INSTRUCTIONS AND WILL PROBABLY BE
TURNED BACK TO TACOMA. WILL DELAY CALLING CREW 5, NO 144,
EXTRA TFR CREW 8, NO 137, NO 149 AND EXTRA TFR CREW 11.
THIRD SUB DIV WORK TRAIN NO 53994 WILL BE CALLED ON DUTY AT
CENTRALIA AT 9AM INSTEAD OF 6AM TO RUN TO BALMER TO HANDLE
PILE DRIVER AND BALLASTCARS TO CENTRALIA TO BE ON HAND CASTLE
ROCK MONDAY OCT 10 FOR BRIDGE REPAIRS AT BRIDGE 86

U S COAST GUARD NOTIFIED DUE TO OIL SPILLAGE FROM FUEL TANKS OF
DERAILED UNITS, NTSB WASH. DC AND SEATTLE NOTIFIED AS WELL AS
ALL BN OFFICERS WITH PRIMARY RESPONSIBILITY FOR RERAILING, TRACK
REPAIRS, PERSONAL AND FREIGHT CLAIMS COMMUNICATIONS AND SIGNAL
REPAIRS AND INSTALLATION
WILL BE NECESSARY TO USE WESTWARD TRACK FOR ALL TRAFFIC UNTIL
EASTWARD CLEAR AND CONFIRMING PHONE MR FLEMING WILL ARRANGE
FOR TELEGRAPH OPERATOR TO BE PUT IN SERVICE AT KENT TO HANDLE
REVERSE TRACK ORDERS. NOW EXPECT EASTWARD TRACK TO BE OPEN
LATE PM TODAY.   CN-90

          DHB
END

movement against the current of traffic. One mistake was all it took to cause far reaching havoc in railroading, including uncertain futures for some of the men who were badly injured.

82. The wreck of trains 143 and 138. *Photo, Jack Flagg.*

RAIL TALES

PLOWING SNOW ON STAMPEDE PASS
By A. H. Wirachowsky - Auburn, Washington

About 1960, I was the engineer on a Northern Pacific Railway snow plowing train on the west side of the mountain between Old Stampede and New Stampede. It was in the late afternoon, but not quite dark. Our train was about a hundred yards from the big tunnel when suddenly the snow on our left side, (the firemen's side of the engine) began to shimmer, and WHOOSH as we were hit by a snowslide. It hit so hard that it derailed the caboose and our train was blocked solid with snow from engine to caboose. As we had the windows open on the engine, the snow came right through and almost filled the cab and of course piled up all around the outside of the engine at the same time. Luckily for us, there was a cat skinner on duty and his cat was warmed up, so the Trainmaster-Roadmaster Bob Robey, who was with us, called for his assistance to re-rail the caboose.

While that was taking place, my fireman, Hubert (Mac) McClinchey, and I started to dig as much of the snow out from in front of the engine as we could. By the time the caboose was re-railed, Mac and I had about three feet of leeway in front of the engine. We conferred with Mr. Robey and the train crew and decided to try to punch our way through the slide to the big tunnel.

We were only ten minutes ahead of passenger train No. 2 when we finally broke through the snow barrier. Our train was put into the siding at Martin on the east end of Stampede Tunnel to clear No. 2. A few days after this workout, the train crew and engine crew received a letter of commendation from Trainmaster Bob Robey. I must add that Trainmaster Robey was a gentleman to work with.

70. NP Rotary 10 on Stampede Pass. *Photo, J.M. Fredrickson*

67. Rotary 10 on Lester turntable, Feb. 1949. *Photo, Albert Farrow.*

48. Lester Depot. *Photo Dallas Barnard.*

RAIL TALES

FIRE AND SNOW AT LESTER DEPOT

By Doug Hubert - Darrington, Washington

I was working the third trick operator job at Lester, Washington on the west side of Stampede Pass on the Old Tacoma Division of the Northern Pacific Railway during the winter of 1968-1969.

It was about 9:30 at night when I wandered downstairs to the agent's office (I slept upstairs in the old Agent's living quarters.) Second trick and I chatted a bit before he went upstairs to fix some dinner in the kitchen. About 10:00 p.m. he came downstairs and told me that the upstairs was on fire.

So, I got on the dispatcher's phone and said, "Dispatcher Lester." Duke Tone was working the second trick mountain dispatcher job and was a very easy-going, hard to excite dispatcher.

He answered, "Dispatcher."

I said, "The depot is on fire!"

He replied, "All right, okay," in a calm voice.

I told Duke we'd wake up "Shorty," the Mexican section foreman, and would let him (Duke) know when the fire was out.

The second trick operator bundled up good, as a blizzard was putting close to a foot of snow an hour on the ground and the wind was coming off Stampede Pass at about twenty miles per hour.

In about fifteen minutes, Shorty and the second trick operator returned with fire axes and fire hose to fight the fire. The chimney from the waiting room stove went up between the corner walls of the upstairs bedroom, where the fire was.

In about thirty minutes Shorty and second trick had the fire out, and just in time too. No more than had they put the last flame out than the fire hose froze solid.

I got on the dispatcher's phone again and told Duke the fire was out and that we would be without heat, as Shorty advised not to use the waiting room stove.

The rotary out of Auburn with Roadmaster Robey was coming after midnight, so I asked Duke if Roadmaster Robey

52. Doug Hubert at Model Railroad Show in 1993, Seattle, Washington. *Photo, Ed Eckes.*

would have coffee and sandwiches sent up for me on the rotary. Duke said the roadmaster agreed to bring food.

Midnight arrived and I bundled up with a T-shirt, wool shirt, sweater and heavy jacket. By the time the rotary arrived, I was cold and hungry. To give you an idea of how cold, there was ice 1/8 inch thick on the inside of the bay window of the depot.

The rotary made a trip over Stampede on the westward main to clear the track; the wind was still howling and snow still falling close to a foot an hour.

Westbound trains were getting red blocks all the way to Lester from Stampede. It seemed like I'd just get warm, then I'd have to go outside and hang orders for either eastbound or westbound trains. This persisted all morning at about one hour intervals.

Finally daylight came and the wind and snow let up somewhat. No. 25, the westbound North Coast Limited now running extra because it was so far behind schedule, headed into the House track behind the depot to let a couple of hotshot westbound freights pass. I had called No. 25's conductor on the radio and told him my situation at the depot and asked if the dining car chef could fix me some breakfast.

He said, "Sure."

So when No. 25 took the House track, I casually walked out the back door of the depot, mounted the steps into the train and got my breakfast.

Second trick was starting his rest days and took No. 25 into Seattle that morning, which left me as the sole employee available for duty. The agent, Kenny Bell, had left the previous day with his family for two weeks vacation and the relief operator, Jerry Schmoe, was on a mail run to Enumclaw. (We found out later that he got stuck in a snow drift and was gone two days before he was found alive but cold and hungry). So I worked on a "call" basis until second trick returned in two days.

I tried to grab some sleep in my sleeping bag, laid out on the agent's desk. When second trick returned, we shared a twenty-four hour day for four days.

No. 25 continued to take the House track each morning for a week. When January 1, 1969, arrived, I climbed on No. 25 and went home to Seattle. I'd had about six hours sleep from Christmas Eve 'till New Years Day!

I wired Chief Dispatcher C. G. Stillman I would be returning to college at Ellensburg, which made this my last shift at Lester after working the job since the previous spring. It was an experience to remember.

NEAR VADER, WASHINGTON - 1918

By Martha Doros - Auburn, Washington

I was born in 1912. In 1918 I was six years old and our family lived near Vader, Washington along the Northern Pacific Railroad double track main line between Seattle and Portland.

When we were young kids, we had to walk to Vader to get our mail. One day on a mail trip, we came upon a drunk man lying on the tracks, so we just picked him up off the tracks and put him in the weeds. A freight train went by just before we started out, and they had seen him and wondered what was wrong with him. They were backing their train up to investigate and asked us if we had seen him and if we knew what was wrong with him. We said he was just a drunk and that we just picked him up and threw him off the tracks. The engineer looked amazed and said, "You did? Have you ever had a ride on a locomotive?"

We told him, "No we haven't"

He said, "We will give you a ride to Vader, but you have to get off on the other side from the depot so nobody sees you."

We climbed abroad the engine with the train crews help and had our wonderful ride on a real locomotive.

Another time it was my job to get our cows across the track. The lead cow started out very fast headed for the barn. I heard a train coming and knew I would have to think fast, so I grabbed the cow by its neck and hung on. There I was hanging on as tight as I could and the train was coming about fifty miles per hour toward us. I braced my feet to keep the cow from moving closer to the tracks and as the train went by, the trainmen were all waving at me. If I hadn't held that dumb cow, she would have run right out in front of the train!

RAIL TALES

SABOTAGE

By Joe LaPorte - Tacoma, Washington

I was called to work Saturday evening, September 20, 1980 for a train to Wenatchee, Washington. After I got to the Interbay Roundhouse in Seattle, Washington, I was told the call was canceled.

When the details were given, we were told there had been a derailment at Snohomish, Washington and ALL trains were canceled!

The next day I was called for wrecker service, and saw firsthand the mess that had occurred. I heard on the grape-vine that it was a case of sabotage, so I brought a book with me about another derailment in Nevada in 1939 which showed the same evidence this derailment had.

In the Snohomish derailment, five engines and sixteen cars turned on their sides about one mile west of Snohomish. Snohomish County deputy sheriffs at the scene, who didn't want to be identified, said a four-foot section of mainline track was missing. Sabotage was suspected because someone had connected a wire across the gap, preventing the broken-rail alarm from sounding. The Snohomish County sheriff's office also said there were no details on the suspected sabotage but they understood the FBI was investigating.

Brakeman George Diede of Auburn was seriously hurt. He suffered a skull fracture and was in critical condition. Three other trainmen were also injured. The derailed train was not carrying any hazardous material. The derailed flatcars were hauling imported goods, including color television sets and plastic flowers. Also aboard were fur coats.

Law enforcement officers at the wreck said saboteurs may have been trying to derail a train carrying propane and other hazardous material that was scheduled to pass at the time the derailment occurred. This train, however had been delayed.

The same method of sabatage used to derail the "City of San Francisco" passenger train in 1939 was used in this wreck also. A rail jack utilized by the section men was used to move the rail, so as to misalign the rail at the joint. With the spikes taken away, and the nut and spring washer removed from the bolts, the rail was moved out a couple of inches.

The person responsible for this derailment had to know something about railroading. He set the bond wires so that the wires had enough slack, and would stretch far enough for the rail to spread apart and still have a clear signal for approaching trains.

At the time of derailment, the train was traveling about sixty miles per hour, so these was no chance to take any action.

When the City of San Francisco derailed, it had seventeen cars and a three unit engine. The Southern Pacific Railroad claimed it was the most modern of all trains. In this derailment fifteen cars were destroyed and two cars on the rear were left in an upright position.

When I arrived with the wrecker that Sunday, the FBI was looking around and trying to size-up the cause of the wreck. I showed them my book, pointing out the similarities of the two wrecks. It took me a month to get my book back. Later, it was my understanding that a disgruntled Burlington Northern employee caused the mishap.